Nº 2 POT
ARCH

# A WINE-LOVER'S GLASSES

The A.C. Hubbard, Jr. Collection of
Antique English Drinking Glasses and Bottles

*Dedicated by A.C.*

TO PENNEY MY LOVE
and to Our Cherished Children
Hadley, Kimberly, and Crawford

# A WINE-LOVER'S GLASSES

## The A.C. Hubbard, Jr. Collection of
## Antique English Drinking Glasses and Bottles

## Ward Lloyd

RICHARD DENNIS
2000

# ACKNOWLEDGEMENTS

The collector, A.C. Hubbard, Jr., has the pleasant task of acknowledging contributions from many friends in the preparation of this book.

I feel so fortunate to be in such fine company and to have a team of contributors who are the leading authorities in their respective fields. I have been humbled by their knowledge, refreshed by their comments and owe them a special debt of gratitude.

To Ward Lloyd I tender my warmest acknowledgment for taking the overall leadership in organizing and pulling together the varied material in this book. His knowledge of eighteenth century English drinking glasses is exceptional and is reflected in his authorship. His wife, Jo, has greatly assisted him.

Dwight P. Lanmon, former director of both the Winterthur Museum, Garden and Library, and the Corning Museum of Glass, has unselfishly shared his time and knowledge about eighteenth century glass with me and I am grateful for this education as well as his contribution of two chapters in this book. I also thank him for offering me the wonderful yard-of-ale glass.

Special thanks are due to Robert Parker who, in my opinion, is the most knowledgeable wine critic in the world. Bob has enhanced my understanding and appreciation of wine, having given me the pleasure of tasting with him on numerous occasions over nearly 20 years. I am grateful for his kind comments. Bob, Pat, Penney and I have shared some wonderful tastings, dinners, and discussions, and their friendship is particularly important to the two of us.

Appreciation is also expressed to Neil Willcox who furnished much of the text related to antique bottles and who has guided me tirelessly in my pursuit of seventeenth and eighteenth century English wine bottles over the past two years. I could not have assembled nearly as much as I have been fortunate enough to buy without Neil's initiative and counsel. David Burton and Roy Morgan have been generous in advice on the text.

Special thanks are due to Simon Cottle, Director, European Ceramics and Glass, Sotheby's London. Simon has contributed his considerable knowledge of Beilby glasses represented in this book and has been of assistance to me in the auction houses over the past ten years. I am especially appreciative of Simon hosting a reception for the introduction of this book in November, 2000, in London.

I thank Richard Dennis, publisher, for his wisdom, for keeping the various contributors on time, and for his persistence in making my dream a reality.

There are several antique glass dealers to whom I owe special thanks. Tony Werneke, from whom I bought my first glass and thereafter most of my glasses for the first six years, has become a close friend. He has spent endless hours explaining the fine points of English glass and his reviewing with me of hundreds of these glasses has been most valuable in helping me build my knowledge base.

Alan Milford has been the primary source for my Collection in recent years and to him I particularly express my great indebtedness. Alan's vast knowledge of eighteenth century glass and ability to locate rare specimens has greatly enhanced the quality of my Collection. He has a unique eye and the confidence of 35 years of experience in the business.

To Martin Mortimer and Tim Osborne go my heartfelt thanks for enabling me to purchase my finest glass, the Royal Dutch Beilby.

I especially appreciate the excellent quality of the photography in this book. The primary photographers were Magnus Dennis and David Brook, who spent five days in my house last February photographing the Collection as well as an Oenarchs' wine dinner.

On a special project basis Rolf Sinclair and Sarah Richards were very helpful in photographing close-up a number of the antique wine bottle seals.

Finally, I am most appreciative of the work of John Dean, who on very short notice took most of the photographs of the individual wine bottles. I also thank Kay Berney for her assistance in computerizing my wine and wine glass inventory and for her diligence and skill in proof-reading this document.

A special tribute to members of our wine-tasting group, the Oenarchs. Beside myself, the group includes Bert Basignani, Dr Hank Dudley, John Mantes, Dr. Jay Miller, Mark Nichols, Robert Parker, and Lee Kirby-Smith. The Oenarchs have been in existence for about ten years and every year each member is responsible for hosting a dinner where the wines are served double blind. The objective of the evening is to guess the theme of the wines with the host providing clues as he sees fit. Some of my most memorable wine experiences have occurred at these dinners and I have greatly valued the friendships established with these gentlemen.

I cannot end my comments of appreciation without acknowledging our glass group, including Dwight and Lorri Lanmon, Julius and Ann Kaplan, Harald and Nancy Leuba, and Penney and A.C. Hubbard. Dwight and Lorri got us together over five years ago at their home for lunch and subsequently we have visited each other's collections on several occasions. You have all shown kindness, hospitality and most importantly friendship to Penney and me. You are the greatest.

Print, design and reproduction by Flaydemouse, Yeovil, Somerset

Published by Richard Dennis, The Old Chapel, Shepton Beauchamp, Somerset TA19 0LE, England © A.C. Hubbard 2000

ISBN 0 903685 81 7

# CONTENTS

| | |
|---|---|
| INTRODUCTION | 7 |
| A.C.'S CELLAR AND THE OENARCHS *by Robert M. Parker, Jr.* | 9 |
| AN OENARCHS' DINNER CHEZ HUBBARD | 14 |
| IN THE BEGINNING | 15 |
| HOW A.C. BEGAN COLLECTING | 15 |
| THE DRAW OF COLLECTING – THE LUCK OF THE DRAW | 16 |
| AN ACADEMIC VIEW | |
| AN INTRODUCTION TO EIGHTEENTH CENTURY ENGLISH DRINKING GLASSES *by Dwight P. Lanmon* | 18 |
| A COTERIE OF GLASS COLLECTORS | 22 |
| A TASTE FOR BALUSTERS | 23 |
| AN APPRECIATION OF BALUSTERS *by Dwight P. Lanmon* | 24 |
| THE DISCONTENTED MR. GREEN | 27 |
| GIANTS AMONG THE GREAT | 28 |
| SOME VARIANTS OF SIZE AND SHAPE | 28 |
| THE RARER KNOPS AND BOWLS | 34 |
| GLASSMAKING MADE EASY – BALUSTROIDS AND PLAIN STEMS | 34 |
| SHORT-LIVED SIMPLE FORMS – INCISED TWISTS AND HOLLOW STEMS | 34 |
| NEWCASTLES – NEW SKILLS | 38 |
| GREAT QUANTITY FROM SMALL MEASURE | |
| SOME SPECULATIONS ON GEORGIAN DRINKING HABITS | 40 |
| RATAFIAS – AN EXAMPLE OF TINY BOWL SIZE | 41 |
| AT A TWIST OF THE BREATH | 41 |
| SEWING THREADS INTO THE STEM – 'COTTON TWISTS' – MULTIPLE DESIGNS IN DRAWN ENAMEL | 46 |
| RINGING THE CHANGES | 49 |
| COLOUR TWISTS | |
| THE PINNACLE OF THE ART | 52 |
| THE SWEETEST OF SWEETMEATS | 61 |
| FACETS – THE CUTTER COMES INTO HIS OWN | 61 |
| GLASS IN THE HANDS OF THE PAINTER – DECORATORS AND DECORATING – THE BEILBYS AND OTHERS | 67 |
| WILLIAM BEILBY AND THE ART OF GLASS PAINTING *by Simon Cottle* | 67 |
| THE KING OF A.C.'S CASTLE – THE DUTCH ROYAL ARMORIAL GOBLET | 70 |
| THE BEST LOVED OF THE FAMILY | 72 |
| THE BRUSH IN DIFFERENT HANDS | 77 |
| THE JACOBITES: THEIR FAMILY AND FRIENDS... | 80 |
| ...AND THEIR ENEMIES | 84 |
| THE ORANGE CONNECTION | 85 |
| SQUARE STEMS FOR A SQUARE KING | 90 |
| PUTTING A NAME ON IT | 91 |
| DECORATING FOR OTHER REASONS | 93 |
| WISHING THEM LUCK | 93 |
| TO SEA IN SHIPS | 95 |
| BACCHUS | 97 |
| UNUSUAL DECORATIVE DEVICES AND OTHER NOVELTIES | 99 |
| BLOWING RASPBERRIES – PRUNTS | 99 |
| MEASURING THE MESS – YARDS AND HALF-YARDS OF ALE | 100 |
| THE PLEASURE OF RUINING YOUR GUESTS' CLOTHES – TRICK GLASSES | 100 |
| WHAT DO YOU KEEP IT IN? | 101 |
| SETTING THE SEAL ON IT – WINE AND THE GLASS BOTTLE | 102 |
| PUTTING A CORK IN IT | 104 |
| POURING WITH ELEGANCE, SERVING BOTTLES | 104 |
| HAD TO HAVES | 116 |
| OUT OF THE BOTTLE – DECANTERS AND CLARET JUGS | 119 |
| OF CANDLESTICKS AND KINGS – AND DECANTERS TOO | 120 |
| EPILOGUE | 126 |
| LIST OF CORKSCREW ILLUSTRATIONS | 127 |

**Fig. 1** *Robert M. Parker, Jr. and A.C. Hubbard, Jr. enjoying their wine from fine baluster glasses at an Oenarchs' Dinner.*

# INTRODUCTION

Though the book which follows is mainly about glass, the inspiration for it comes from A.C. Hubbard Jr. – the man and his love of wine. It is A.C. who has provided the enthusiasm for collecting, the expertise on wine, many of the anecdotes, and above all the splendid glasses, bottles and wine related articles that we illustrate and discuss here. I and my friends and learned colleagues Dwight Lanmon, Simon Cottle, Neil Willcox and in particular Alan Milford, and Richard Dennis, our publisher, merely supplied the academic knowledge and the experience we have gained from a combined total of one hundred and fifty years or more we have spent in studying and handling antique glass – principally the English drinking glasses of the seventeenth and eighteenth centuries which form the greater part of the superb Hubbard Collection, published here for the first time. A.C. has asked me to express special appreciation of Robert Parker's expert contribution on the subject of wine itself.

We all want this book to be more than just a catalogue of fine individual pieces of antique glass. We hope that by presenting the comprehensive Collection in all its splendour we will draw attention to a neglected field of eighteenth century art – English glass. These artifacts have too long been unrecognised for what they are – examples of the best of English domestic design in its heyday, at a pinnacle never before reached or subsequently surpassed. Many of them, both in shape and decoration, are works of art in their own right, but one should remember that they were made for a practical purpose, and their decoration – engraving, gilding, painting, etc. – however technically and artistically stunning, remains secondary to their basic design. So also is their use as vehicles for political or factional statements, gifts and love tokens, satire, commemorations and aggrandisement (in the form of family crests and armorials – which were occasionally the inventions of the nouveaux riches!). First and foremost, they were crafted as drinking vessels in the appropriate style of the day, sometimes of special shape and size such as ratafias, cordials, toast-master glasses and

so on, but in the main they were designed for the consumption of fine wines. Chiefly, these were claret and port – the gentleman's drinks – but also of course burgundies, hocks and champagne (curiously, apparently flat, since it was sometimes decanted), virtually all, you will note, with the exception of the fortified wines – sherry, port, madeira, marsala, etc. – coming from France or certain areas of what is now Germany. (There are of course notable exceptions, such as Tokay).

Practical and blending superbly with the fashions and decorations of their time, the designs of wine glasses and glassware make a statement of their right to be recognised along with furniture, silver and other metals, ceramics, carpets and curtains, wallpaper and paint, and so on, as a high-point of eighteenth century English applied art.

A.C. was inspired to acquire these glasses not only for their beauty of shape and decoration and the manner in which they reflect their time in English history, but more particularly for the way they complement his Collection of great wines – his love which is well exemplified by the fact that even his yellow labrador is named for the grape. She is called Châteauneuf du Pape (more affectionately Poppy) after one of his favourite wine regions. His entrepreneurial style and boundless energy has helped him to assemble all these pieces (presently about five hundred specimens) in less than twelve years. Indeed, it was his love of the pursuit of these objects and his willingness to take risks in regards to their authenticity and price that made it possible for him to gather together so many exceptional pieces in such a relatively short period. Additionally, this is a living and growing Collection which will continue to expand. Eventually, virtually all will go back to the marketplace, so as to enable another generation of antique glass collectors to enjoy the hunt as much as A.C. has.

*Ward Lloyd*

N.B. American spelling is used where the writer is American, otherwise spelling is in the English manner.

**Fig. 2** *Wise words from John Blades, on an eighteenth century paper label for packed glass – relevant then as it is today.*
© Copyright The British Museum

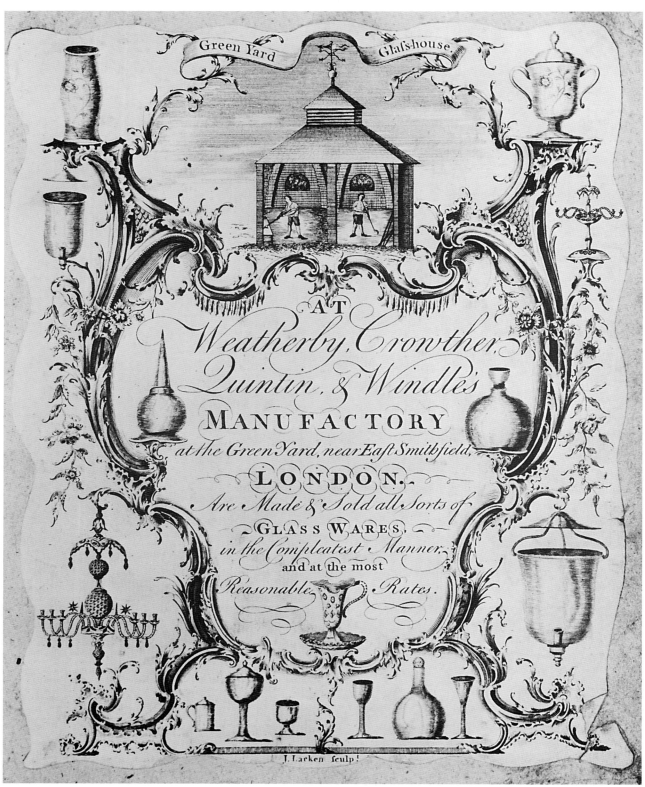

**Fig. 3** *It is interesting to speculate that some of the beautiful glasses in the Collection may have originated from this very glasshouse or from other houses whose magnificent eighteenth century trade cards are illustrated in this book. We shall never know for sure, but it seems more than likely that some of the Collection started here, since these are leading glassmakers of their day and A.C.'s glasses are all outstanding examples of the craft. © Copyright The British Museum.*

# A.C.'S CELLAR AND THE OENARCHS

## by Robert M. Parker, Jr.

I suppose it is no surprise that the first time I met A.C. Hubbard, Jr. was at a wine tasting. If my recollection is correct, it was in 1981 at a vertical tasting of Robert Mondavi's Reserve Cabernet Sauvignon. What struck me about A.C. then was his passion and enthusiasm for wine. It was inevitable that such passion would inspire this book. A.C. Hubbard, Jr.'s interest in wine extends beyond reading and tasting. He also possesses a form of zealotry when it comes to the pursuit of information about antique wine glasses and decanters. While I am not qualified to comment on the quality and scope of A.C.'s Collection (it is certainly the most impressive I have encountered), I am comfortably prepared to talk about our friendship over the last nineteen years, his inclusion in a wine tasting group called Les Oenarchs, and his impeccable wine cellar.

I have gotten to know A.C. well through the blind wine tastings hosted by the eight members of the group we call Les Oenarchs. This group was formed a decade ago as a derivative and homage to a group of great wine lovers from Bordeaux called *Les Oenarques*. For more than a decade on my frequent trips to Bordeaux, I have been a privileged guest at their blind wine tastings, which have included just about every memorable Bordeaux vintage − 1921, 1926, 1928, 1929, 1947, 1948, 1959, 1961, 1982 and 1990. Our group is modelled after *Les Oenarques* of Bordeaux (in 1998, one of the French Oenarchs, Bernard Ginestet, wrote a detailed, very sentimental book about their tasting exploits and comradeship, called *La Memoire des Oenarques*). The eight French Oenarchs include four superb private collectors, Roger Bessières, Henri Boyreau, Jacques Debayle and Georges Chambarière, and four members of the Bordeaux wine trade, Jean-Bernard Dolmas (the administrator of Haut-Brion, La Mission-Haut-Brion, and La Tour-Haut-Brion), Jean-François Moueix (owner of Château Pétrus, and president of several negotiant firms), Bernard Ginestet (whose family once owned Château Margaux, but who spends most of his time editing and writing books), and Pierre Casteja (another château proprietor). The purpose of their tastings, which we copied, is for each of the eight members to alternate hosting a blind tasting based on a single theme. The tasting is arranged around a fine meal. Of course, the fun is the guessing game of trying to not only determine what the wine vintages are, but what is the theme of the tasting. In addition to A.C. Hubbard, Jr., our eight members include John Mantis (a Maryland wine wholesaler), Dr. Jay Miller and Mark Nichols (both representatives of local wine wholesalers), Bertero Basignani (a Maryland winery owner), Dr. Albert Dudley, III (an orthopedic surgeon, and member of another wine tasting group called The Wine and Spine Society), Lee Kirby-Smith (a specialist in high-tech music and television apparatus), and me (a lowly wine critic). Our tastings have ranged from simple verticals of renowned California Cabernets (i.e. Joseph Phelps' Insignia, Dunn's Howell Mountain, Château Montelena, Beaulieu's Private Reserve, Ridge

**Fig. 4** *Great wines, great glasses... the subdued splendour of A.C.'s cellar.*

Monte Bello), to horizontal tastings of Zinfandel, 1974, 1976, and 1978 North Coast California Cabernet Sauvignons, 1982 Bordeaux, verticals of famous Bordeaux châteaux (Latour, Lynch Bages), horizontals of 1990 Châteauneuf du Pape, and verticals of famous wines such as Spain's Vega Sicilia. No one has kept an official scorecard of who has guessed the most vintages and identified the most wines, but I suspect I am in second place following Dr. Jay Miller, who has a nearly flawless record of unearthing the 'key' to these themed tastings, and identifying so many vintages and individual wines correctly. Of course A.C. has been part of our fun and games and has hosted some of our most memorable tastings, not surprising in view of his wine cellar.

It is hard to describe A.C.'s wine cellar other than to say it is an underground vault, beautifully appointed, meticulously organised, and crammed with liquid gems. Readers would probably find it hard to say he has a bias in favor of this style or type of wine versus another, but his cellar contains copious quantities of French wines, particularly Burgundy and Bordeaux. Not surprisingly, given his Collection of historic sherry and port crystal, there is also a wealth of classic vintage ports in this vinous treasure trove. It seems to me that A.C. has been purchasing more and more Rhône wines over the last years, and, with a handful of exceptions (Marcassin and Harlan Estate being the most notable), has tended to shy away from the high end California designer wines. He also does not appear to be a huge fan of Italy's gems, yet I have spotted some Italian classics in his cellar (namely Sassicaia). Perhaps there is just not enough room for everything. Nevertheless, he seems to be primarily a Francophile, with an increasing interest in the great wines of the Rhône.

A.C. Hubbard's Oenarch tastings have always tantalised our group. We all tend to have a good working knowledge of the contents of our members' cellars, which actually tends to be a disadvantage in trying to figure out what they are trying to do at our blind tastings. Several years ago, his tasting/dinner was held at Baltimore's finest restaurant, Charleston. He surprised everyone with a brilliant tasting of old Burgundies, including pristine and sumptuous bottles of Leroy's 1964 Echèzeaux, Grand Echèzeaux, and Romanée St. Vivant competing for attention with the Domaine de la Romanée-Conti's 1964 La Tache, Grands Echèzeaux, and Richebourg. Talk about a challenge of the Titans! That dinner was matched on A.C.'s subsequent turn with two verticals at the same tasting, Rayas 1978-1990 and Jaboulet's Hermitage La Chapelle 1959-1990. Moreover, the extravagant decadence of this evening was further enhanced by the fact that we rinsed our palates with the 1991, 1992 and 1993 Marcassin Gauer Vineyard Chardonnay before we attacked the reds! Most recently, he somehow managed to

**Fig 5**  *The glories of Château d'Yquem. The great vintages from 1967-1990 glow deeper with age in A.C.'s cellar.*

find enough bottles of the famed Australian wine, Penfold's Grange Hermitage, to put on another extraordinary tasting. Following a palate cleaner of magnums of the 1969 and 1964 Krug, he launched into the first flight, which no one seemed to have a problem analyzing – the Montrachets of Domaine de la Romanée-Conti. The question was, which vintages? We tasted the 1989, 1986 and 1983 – and all of them performed magnificently well. However, the themed part of the tasting, which is almost always 10-12 red wines, was a vertical of Penfold's Grange Hermitage starting in 1989 and ending in 1955. There were no disappointments in these virtually perfect wines, which included the 1971 1976, 1982, and 1986. I'll go to my grave happy if I can taste just one more time in my life the 1971 and 1976! We finished the night with an extraordinary pristine bottle of 1948 Taylor. A.C., with his world-class collection of antique port glasses, probably has an unequaled quantity of 1948 Taylor and 1948 Fonseca squirreled away for showing off these exquisite glasses.

A.C. Hubbard Jr., the person, is, like his wine and glass collection, someone of extraordinary generosity. It is his spirit of sharing, his passion for learning, and his impeccable attention to detail that undoubtedly compelled him to want to write this book. It is an honor for me to offer these brief insights into his passion for wine and glassware, and his contributions as a member of our wine tasting group, Les Oenarchs. I'm sure readers will be enchanted by his perspective of wine, glassware, and the cultivated art he has perfected in pursuing his passions.

*Robert M. Parker, Jr.*
*Monkton, Maryland*
*July, 2000*

**Fig 6** *The entrance to A.C.'s cellar is lined with crate-ends from some of his favourite wines.*

**Plate 2** *Neil Willcox comments: These examples date: circa 1730, 1740, 1750, 1790, plus two unique English-made 'boot' forms of the late eighteenth century. The style is known from German imports of the 1760-80 period, but these are the first British made specimens I have encountered. In all my experience, since the days when early bottles were lotted in wine sales as 'relics', the sale which included this grouping – held by Sotheby's in September 1999 – stands out. This 'house sale', removed from a property in Scotland, included items such as these. To quote Sotheby's ..."some objects still stood where first placed, most notably, the eighteenth century wine bottles in the cellar ...".*

**Plate 1** *Neatly linking A.C.'s cellar with the antique wine bottles which he collects are these château bottles of the nineteenth century, which will lead us back in due course to fabulous, much earlier specimens such as plate 2.*

**Fig 7** *These are a find of considerable significance to the story of a 'wine interest' collection. In this day and age, it is truly exceptional to find undisturbed such a grouping of eighteenth century bottles with original contents, corks, and cork sealing. The cylinder shape of the late eighteenth century exhibits the original string binding of the protruding cork. This is the only surviving example I know of with this binding. On British military fort sites in the West Indies, I have come across such circa 1800 blown cylinder bottle necks with copper wire still in place, the cork long disintegrated - clearly 'cracked off'.* Sotheby's, London.

11

**Fig. 8** *The red wine decanted for the Oenarchs' February, 2000 wine tasting dinner.*

**Fig. 9** *A Georgian London wine establishment – Gray's Inn. In the eighteenth and nineteenth centuries much wine for private consumption would have been bottled and corked at the merchant, as illustrated on this trade card. Guildhall Library, Corporation of London.*

**Fig. 10** *This miracle of miniaturisation was created as a sixtieth birthday present for A.C. by his gifted sister-in-law, Anne Hubbard. Its dimensions are 34ins long by 19ins wide by 9½ins high. It is made on a scale of one inch to one foot, and shows tiny glasses, furniture and bottles, exactly duplicating those in A.C.s Collection on a Lilliputian scale. I tell the following, to give some idea of its accuracy: although I had not seen it, I had been told of the existence of this model and came across a photograph of it among other illustrations for this book. Although the intention was to include a picture of it, I examined this under a magnifying glass and discarded it under the illusion that it showed the actual cellar itself.*

**Fig. 11** *A contemporary wooden sculpture by Pello Irazu from A.C.'s Collection with selected miniature glasses from the eighteenth century.*

**Plate 3** *Apart from some great giant glasses, A.C. is putting together a collection of miniature wine glasses and decanters.*

# AN OENARCHS' DINNER CHEZ HUBBARD

A.C. speaks fondly of this notable meal which he hosted in October 1999. The chef responsible for preparing the feast was Arthur Leech of the Range Restaurant in Jackson, Wyoming. In addition to the meal itself, A.C. spent three most enjoyable days with Arthur, first in discussing and deciding which wines would match the food (a particular pleasure for A.C.), then in finding the ingredients and watching their preparation. The really hard task for Arthur was to choose and prepare the main courses in order to stand up to the intensity of the Penfold's Grange Hermitage which was to be served with them, but all the guests agreed he had met the challenge superbly. The menu and wine list are appended. Of the twelve vintages of Penfold's poured, the 1971 and the 1976 were most favoured. The 1955 vintage was included for its academic value (this being the first year that Penfold's Grange declared a vintage), but it is interesting to note that those present still thought it deserved the 85 out of 100 point rating it received by the wine critics.

**Fig. 12** *The Oenarch's in A.C.'s wine cellar in October, 1999. They began the wine tasting with a magnum of 1969 Krug Collection champagne. Photograph by Penney Hubbard.*

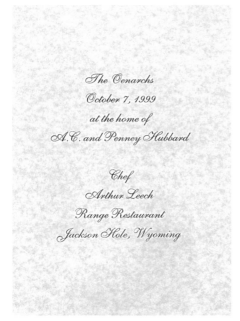

The Oenarchs

October 7, 1999

at the home of

A.C. and Penney Hubbard

Chef

Arthur Leech

Range Restaurant

Jackson Hole, Wyoming

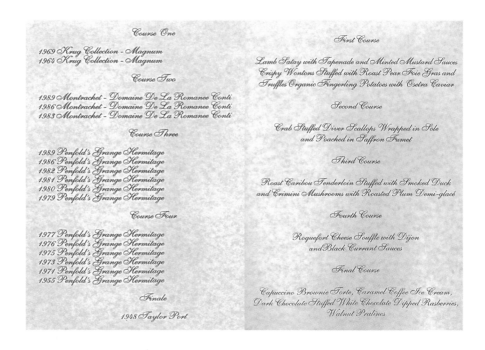

Course One

1969 Krug Collection - Magnum
1964 Krug Collection - Magnum

Course Two

1989 Montrachet - Domaine De La Romanee Conti
1986 Montrachet - Domaine De La Romanee Conti
1983 Montrachet - Domaine De La Romanee Conti

Course Three

1989 Penfold's Grange Hermitage
1986 Penfold's Grange Hermitage
1982 Penfold's Grange Hermitage
1981 Penfold's Grange Hermitage
1980 Penfold's Grange Hermitage
1979 Penfold's Grange Hermitage

Course Four

1977 Penfold's Grange Hermitage
1976 Penfold's Grange Hermitage
1975 Penfold's Grange Hermitage
1973 Penfold's Grange Hermitage
1971 Penfold's Grange Hermitage
1955 Penfold's Grange Hermitage

Finale

1948 Taylor Port

First Course

Lamb Satay with Tapenade and Minted Mustard Sauces
Crispy Wontons Stuffed with Roast Pear Foie Gras and
Truffles Organic Fingerling Potatoes with Osetra Caviar

Second Course

Crab Stuffed Diver Scallops Wrapped in Sole
and Poached in Saffron Fumet

Third Course

Roast Caribou Tenderloin Stuffed with Smoked Duck
and Crimini Mushrooms with Roasted Plum Demi-glacé

Fourth Course

Roquefort Cheese Souffle with Dijon
and Black Currant Sauces

Final Course

Capuccino Brownie Torte, Caramel Coffee Ice Cream,
Dark Chocolate Stuffed White Chocolate Dipped Rasberries,
Walnut Pralines

**Fig. 13.** *The Oenarchs' dinner. 1999.*

# IN THE BEGINNING

## HOW A.C. BEGAN COLLECTING

Not many people recognise the important part played by antique glass in Georgian design and manners. Fine art, furniture, porcelain etc, are all much better understood. Even the Hubbards, with their highly developed appreciation for the beauty of the past (as well as a taste for fine food and wine) came on glass only by chance. Fortunately their cultivated eyes immediately realised that they had stumbled on something remarkable. Others have not been so lucky – or inspired. Hence, the glaring anachronisms in the glass of antique interiors and table settings presented in supposedly correct period backgrounds for drama, film and television. Were the same to occur with, say, costume or furnishings, the production companies would be deluged with complaints. In the case of glass, the only antique style on offer seems to be at best Edwardian, regardless of date. Thus cut crystal of 1910 or so is shown in the hands of every reasonably prosperous person throughout the ages. It is worth mentioning in passing that our publisher, Richard Dennis, irritated (as I am) by these persistent errors, started a business which offered for hire to film companies and the like, good reproductions of glass (principally drinking glasses) covering the seventeenth, eighteenth and nineteenth centuries. There were few takers, since the public is largely ignorant or indifferent, and the company closed in 1970.

A.C.'s abiding interest in Georgian drinking glasses arose quite fortuitously. Romanesque and Gothic cathedrals had long fascinated the Hubbards. In their study of these and similar architectural marvels, they were

**Fig. 14** *Mompesson House, Salisbury, England.*

advised by a close friend, Dr. Robert Bergman (now sadly deceased), formerly head of the Walters Gallery in Baltimore and the Cleveland Museum. He would suggest buildings to be visited by the Hubbards while they were travelling in Europe, and it was because of his expert guidance that they found themselves in Salisbury, viewing the beautiful cathedral there. On leaving the building and crossing the cathedral close, they came upon Mompesson House, a National Trust property which has a fine collection of eighteenth century English glass, the Turnbull collection. They were deeply impressed by the great beauty of the glass objects they saw displayed there, and spent an enthralling hour or so viewing them, assuming that these were extremely rare – quite possibly unique. They never expected to see their like again. It was close to a year later that they encountered Tony Werneke. As one of the major dealers at the Hunt Valley Antiques Show, he had on display about fifty eighteenth century English drinking glasses. Much discussion ensued, with Tony generously contributing a mass of background information on the subject and convincing A.C. that it was still quite possible to acquire specimens as fine as he had seen in Salisbury. The upshot of this was the purchase of the first glass to grace the Hubbard. Collection – a double series twist with dimple-moulded bowl.

That summer in London, A.C. and his wife Penney – with her parents – visited Delomosne, the well-known Kensington glass dealer, now removed to the West Country. There A.C. bought two more glasses – never guessing that from this beginning would quickly grow a splendid collection of five hundred or more superb

15

examples of antique glass, and wine-related items, acquired over the next twelve years. His appetite had been whetted, and as his knowledge increased so his Collection grew.

## THE DRAW OF COLLECTING – THE LUCK OF THE DRAW

We have already noted A.C.'s application to collecting – his determination to have only the best examples within the limits he had set himself. It might not be out of place also to comment on his luck! It so happened that two major collectors of English glass died at just about the time that he was assembling the core of his Collection. One of these was Clive Quie, an avid collector in many fields of antiques, although he was almost unknown outside of the major auction houses and the trade. The other was the well-known barrister, Michael Parkington. Apart from their mutual passion for collecting, both men were larger than life and deserving of detailed bibliographies to tell their fascinating stories. However, our concern is obviously with their glass collections. That of Parkington was huge. My wife and I were privileged to assist in forming it. A large part was donated to Broadfield House Glass Museum, but enough rare and beautiful pieces remained to form a three-part sale at Christies. From this, A.C. acquired some choice examples of early English glass. The Quie Collection was assembled for him over a period of twenty years by my friend and colleague Alan Milford, whose wide experience and knowledge enabled Clive to form a truly magnificent and valuable collection – containing examples of the finest and best of eighteenth century English glasses, particularly colour twists and commemorative goblets. With Alan's help, A.C. was able to obtain the bulk of these pieces. Obviously, the fact that so many good glasses – in particular those of Clive Quie – became available, was helpful in expanding the Collection at a time when A.C. had already begun to add extensively to it, aided by Tony Werneke's enthusiasm in the States and Alan's experience in tracing fine glasses in Europe.

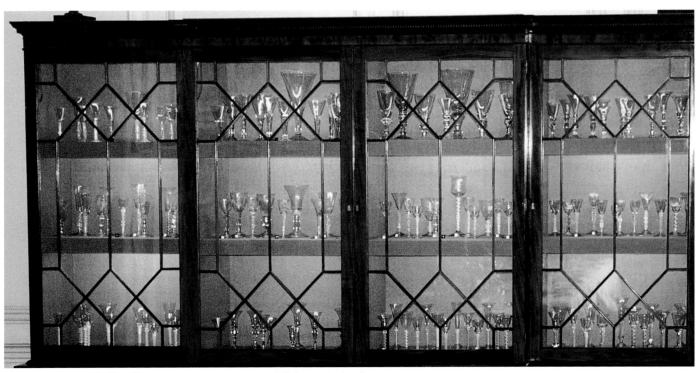

**Fig. 15** *The Turnbull Collection, Mompesson House, Salisbury, England.*

**Fig. 16** *Dealer Tony Werneke, Penney Hubbard, and A.C. discussing an eighteenth century wine goblet at the Hunt Valley Antique Show. A.C. bought his first eighteenth century glass from Tony Werneke at the same antique show in February, 1987.*

**Fig. 17** *Guildhall Library, Corporation of London.*

**Fig. 18** *A.C. and Alan Milford, with some of A.C.'s Collection in the background, discuss a privateer decanter – a great rarity. The cotton twist glass is identically inscribed and decanter and glass were recently reunited. The pair to this decanter (engraved CLARET, and damaged) is illustrated in an article in the Burlington Magazine, November 1919 (Sea Power under George III). The inscription, 'Succef to ye Good Intent' seems euphemistic. Privateers' intentions might be anything but good. See page 94.*

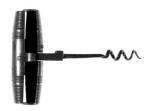

# AN ACADEMIC VIEW
## AN INTRODUCTION TO EIGHTEENTH CENTURY ENGLISH DRINKING GLASSES

### by Dwight P. Lanmon

My wife and I collect eighteenth century English wine glasses, and occasionally we offer after dinner drinks in them. We usually hear, "It's so beautiful! It must be rare and extremely valuable. How do you dare let me use it?" We respond that we think that most eighteenth century English drinking glasses are, indeed, beautiful, but that they are surprisingly easy to find, considering their age and fragility. Handling them with respect is what matters most, and they never go in the dishwasher. And, what a delight it is to drink port from a two-hundred-year-old glass!

Our friends are surprised that it is still possible to acquire fine examples. The reason that they are so available is that many were made – probably hundreds of thousands of glasses were produced in England every year throughout much of the eighteenth century, and large numbers have miraculously survived without a chip or crack. Unlike many collecting fields, where the best pieces entered museum collections long ago and are unavailable, important English glasses dating from the eighteenth century still come on the market. Indeed, that is one important lesson that may be learned from the glasses published in this book – many for the first time. There are many masterpieces in it, yet the entire Collection was formed in about twelve years! He notes that he purchased his first glass in 1987. This shows what is possible, although not all of us have A.C.'s diligence.

The reason that so many drinking glasses were made in England in the eighteenth century is because heavy drinking was common throughout Europe and the English-speaking world. The upper classes drank strong ale, champagne, imported German, French and Portuguese wines, cordials and brandy. Beer and cider, often home brewed, were popular as well. Gin was the drink of the masses due to the ease with which it could be cheaply produced and its freedom from import duty. Thus, gin drinking became widespread in the early eighteenth century and was quickly regarded as a scourge of the English populace. Thomas Fielding observed in

*Tom Jones* in 1750 that "should the drinking of this poison [gin] be continued in its present height during the next twenty years, there will, by that time, be very few of the common people left to drink it". Drunkenness was a significant social problem throughout the eighteenth century, and it was not confined to one class or to men alone. It is estimated that one-eighth of all deaths in London in the early eighteenth century resulted from excessive drinking.

Even in the North American colonies, the amount of liquor consumed at a party would seem prodigious by modern standards, and doubtless many glasses were destroyed every evening. However, great houses in America and England would have had a large supply to replenish those broken in a night's carousing. For example, Lord Botetourt, the Royal Governor of Virginia who died in 1770, had some 1,000 glass serving and drinking vessels in his pantry and 6,000 bottles of liquor in his cellar in the Governor's Palace in Williamsburg. What did they look like? Chances are, the glasses and bottles in this book, dating from around 1770, would have been the types used by Lord Botetourt and his guests.

In the 1650s, drinking glasses in England were thin and fragile, and most were imported from Venice or northern Europe. In the 1670s, a glassmaker named George Ravenscroft found a way to make glass using English raw materials – glass that could compete with imported glass. He aimed at producing something that looked like rock crystal, which was being avidly collected and carved into luxurious vessels in many European royal courts, and which was the standard of clarity for colorless glass made throughout Europe.

Glass is typically made from three common raw materials: silica (usually in the form of sand, but occasionally flints), an alkali (usually potash or soda) that lowers the melting temperature of the silica, and a stabiliser (usually lime) that makes the mixture insoluble in water. Eventually, Ravenscroft developed a new formula which used lead oxide as one of the principal ingredients in addition to silica, potash and lime. Lead glass was not new, but before Ravenscroft made it, it was mainly used to produce artificial gems. The addition of lead oxide had a dramatic effect on the product, the glass had considerable sparkle, it was noticeably heavy, and it rang like a bell when tapped. Ravenscroft called it 'a sort of crystalline glass resembling rock crystal'. He received a patent from the king for the sole right to be the manufacturer of it for seven years.

At first, there were technical problems with the glass, but by the 1680s the formula was perfected, and many glasshouses began using it to produce drinking glasses and other serving and decorative pieces. Lead glass objects were sent to the North American colonies in quantity, and by the 1690s most table glass used in America was made in England. Indeed, within twenty years of its perfection, the most fashionable table glass used throughout the English world was made to the new formula.

The ever-changing fashion in interior decoration influenced the development of a series of new glass styles throughout the eighteenth century, and these styles shifted into something recognisably 'new' about every twenty to thirty years. In the 1680s, the forms of drinking glasses made in England largely emulated the forms of imported Venetian glasses but, because lead glass was much heavier and slower to set, it was difficult to fabricate it into the elaborate *façon-de-Venise* shapes. Therefore, beginning in the late 1690s, a new, simplified style was perfected and became fashionable. It featured glasses on stems with bold, massive, rounded 'knops' (the decorative knobs on the stems) in a variety of forms. The knops displayed the brilliance of the lead glass to perfection, and decorative air

bubbles were often added to enhance it. These substantial glasses related closely to the furniture of the day, and the style lasted until the 1720s. They are called *heavy balusters* by collectors, to denote the massive stems.

Another stem type had a brief vogue toward the end of this period. It was a panel-moulded stem, with either four, six or eight sides. It appeared in England about 1715 and has been associated with German glassmakers, since the style became fashionable when the first Hanoverian king, George I, ascended the English throne. Indeed, the words 'God Save King George' were moulded, a word to each side, on some very rare four-sided stems. The panel-moulded stem was popular for only about a decade or two on drinking glasses, but it remained fashionable much longer on candlesticks and dessert stands (objects that look like cake stands). Dessert stands were arranged in graduated sets of two, three or four, in dramatic pyramidal centre-pieces that were equipped with numerous glasses for jellies and other sweets. Throughout the eighteenth century, there was also a rough-and-tumble style of drinking glass that featured a plain stem, it was frequently ornamented with a single air bubble at the base of the bowl. They were

Bought of John Burroughs at the Glasse house without Ludgate London.

**Fig. 19** *Fire was a constant hazard of glasshouse life. A building of this dramatic design in brick and stone must have seemed real progress. In 1703 purpose-built structures were uncommon. It is interesting to note, however, that the shape of the furnace, the 'glory hole', the pontil rod, the survitors and the gaffer in his chair have scarcely varied since Roman times. Perhaps this accounts for the innate visual and tactile appeal of fine glass, especially that of eighteenth century England which can be enjoyed today in famous displays like those in A.C.'s Collection.* © Copyright The British Museum.

ubiquitous in households across England and in the English colonies in North America and, because they were so sturdy, they were especially popular in taverns. There are slight differences between the earlier and later varieties — mainly in the amount of glass that was used in their production. Initially, the foot was usually folded, but economic necessity caused this to disappear in the interest of lightness.

As the eighteenth century progressed, stems on drinking glasses became less massive and more complex in design. Glasses from the 1720s through to the 1740s

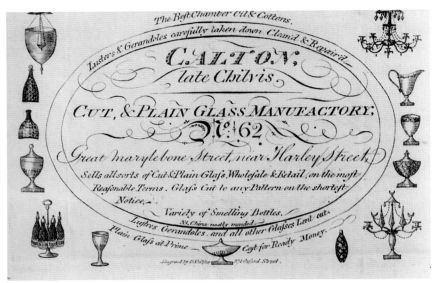

**Fig 20** *An eighteenth century trade card illustrates cut and plain glass, N.B. 'glass cut to any pattern on the shortest notice'. Guildhall Library, Corporation of London.*

are called *balustroid* by collectors – signifying that the knops had become smaller. Toward the end of the period, in the early 1740s, another drinking glass stem also became popular. These stems featured long, thin air bubbles drawn into decorative spirals and are termed *air twists.*

These shifts in glass styles reflected the simultaneous lightening and softening of interior design in the 1720s and 1730s. The new style of furniture featured chairs whose legs tended to be curvilinear and frequently incorporated 'S' shapes. Fashionable rooms were unified ensembles that included ornamental glass, drinking glasses, ceramics, silver of all sorts, lighting devices, and suites of matching furniture. William Hogarth, an artist and printmaker, captured the key elements of the style in the design that he called 'the line of beauty' – a three dimensional, spiral, serpentine line. The spiralling air twist in a wineglass stem is the perfect embodiment of Hogarth's 'line'.

The increasing lightness of the glasses also reflected an economic stimulus – taxation. As England engaged in foreign wars, the government needed to find ways to balance the national budget. One way was to tax manufacturers. Throughout the eighteenth century, the English government levied and gradually increased taxes on the raw materials for glassmaking, inadvertently encouraging the development of lighter, more delicate, and more decorative forms of table glass.

In the late 1740s, another furnishing style became the rage. It originated in France and was called *rococo.* Furniture was decorated with a flurry of curved lines and voluptuous, ornamental carved flowers, birds and figures,

foliage and vines. Much of it was gilded, and the wood used for the rest was the finest mahogany from Central America – preferred to native walnut because it was not subject to woodworm. In America, we call the style *Chippendale,* after the designer and cabinetmaker who published an influential 1754 book of designs depicting furniture in the rococo style.

Air twist glasses suited the new interiors perfectly, and the twists became more and more complex in the 1750s.

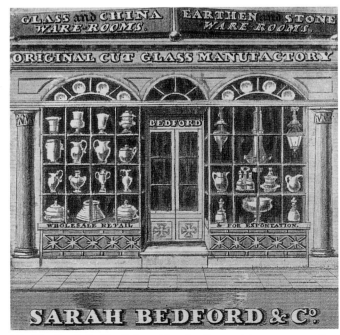

**Fig 21** *Sarah Bedford's humble advertisement is a rare exception to her metropolitan rivals, being situated in Birmingham. Pictures of eighteenth century provincial shop fronts are rare. © Copyright The British Museum.*

**Fig. 22** *Guildhall Library, Corporation of London.*
**Plate 4** *As one might expect, china, glass and Staffordshire earthenware were sold on the same premises. Blue 'Finger cups' are interesting, as are wine glasses with Delph(?) borders and cut bottom tumblers. Relating this invoice to the Collection is one of the few non-glass pieces that the Collection contains – a late Georgian Staffordshire meat platter printed with a scene of grape-pressing.*

Another type of twist stem was also perfected. It incorporated delicate spiral threads of colored glass – usually opaque white but sometimes in brilliant polychrome. Colored threads were also combined with air twists in unusual, elegant, and, unfortunately, very rare and hard-to-find variations.

As you can readily see in the Collection, engraving, gilding or enamelling further decorated many of these rococo glasses. The most elaborate enamelling was done by a brother-and-sister team, William and Mary Beilby, who worked in Newcastle-upon-Tyne in northern England. One of their important works is a large goblet with colored armorial decoration – one of the many treasures of the Collection, see page 71. Wineglasses and other tableware decorated by the Beilbys – chiefly in opaque white enamel – are among the most engaging and delicate glasses made in the rococo style.

Some colored glass was made during this period, but was not often used for drinking glasses – although colored glasses with twist stems and some with colored bowls and feet do exist. Brilliant green, rich blue, and creamy white glass was produced, but mainly for vases, decanters and other tableware. Such pieces were frequently decorated with gilding.

In the 1760s, cutting became popular on drinking glasses, decanters, bowls and other table glass and lighting fixtures. Cutting had been used to ornament expensive glassware in England since the 1710s, or perhaps even earlier, but it did not become a common

form of decoration for another fifty years. It then continued into the style of decorating that succeeded the rococo – the neoclassical style. The excavation of the ancient Roman city of Herculaneum, which began in 1709, and Pompeii in 1748, sparked renewed interest in Roman and Grecian antiquities. Gentlemen who embarked on the Grand Tour of Europe, visiting famous ancient sites and collecting ancient art fuelled this interest. At home, architects like Robert Adam and furniture makers like George Hepplewhite and Thomas Sheraton were building and furnishing houses with rooms that emulated what they had seen. Designs derived from ancient frescoes and stone carvings were used to decorate furniture, walls, carpets, ceramics and other ornamental items. Josiah Wedgwood's famous neoclassical basalt and jasperwares, some reproducing actual ancient pieces, became the rage. Also inspired by this vogue was superb plasterwork on walls and ceilings – often executed by highly skilled imported Italian artisans. Everything in a fashionable neoclassical room was unified in style, from the carved urn on the back of a chair to the low-relief plaster urn on the wall – or even that surrounding the keyhole on a desk.

Glassmakers played their part by making superb chandeliers, candelabra, mirrors and mirror frames, cutting them in increasingly elaborate facets, which caught and refracted light in brilliant rainbows. Square-footed bowls, urns and drinking glasses, designed to imitate neoclassical decorative elements, became common, and elaborately engraved and gilded designs of swags, ox skulls (called bucrania) and floral elements were widely used. Colored glass (transparent blue, green, purple and opaque white) became more common during this period, in part because gilded decoration was so much more striking on a colored ground.

In the nineteenth century, glassmakers produced vast numbers of elaborate designs. There were spectacular, technical *tours-de-force* of cutting, moulding, and other innovations, but the clarity of design evident throughout the eighteenth century was all too often lost in the jumble. By the early nineteenth century, the 'classic' period of English glassmaking had ended.

Dwight P. Lanmon
*Director Emeritus, Winterthur Museum, Garden & Library*
*Former Director, The Corning Museum of Glass*

# A COTERIE OF GLASS COLLECTORS

It was Dwight P. Lanmon, formerly director of the Corning Museum of Glass and recently retired director of Winterthur Museum, Garden and Library, who was chiefly responsible for the formation of the group – an informal gathering of collectors who have come together over the last six years, to share friendship and experiences. A.C. cites this company as providing some of the happiest moments of his life as a collector. The group first met at Chandlers Farm, Winterthur, then the home of Dwight and Lorri Lanmon, subsequent meetings being held at the homes of other members. In addition to the Lanmons, these are (or sadly in the case of the late Tony Stout, were), A.C. and Penney Hubbard, Harald and Nancy Leuba, Jay and Anne Kaplan. Numerous other collectors, dealers and museum representatives have attended gatherings as guests. The friendships formed over the years within the group have allowed the development of strong feelings of respect and helpfulness, while still permitting competitiveness in the marketplace, particularly at auctions. As an example, it was Harald Leuba who alerted A.C. that the great signed Dutch Royal armorial goblet by William Beilby was about to be offered for sale by Delomosne at the June 1998 Ceramics Fair in London. A.C. made the special trip and queued almost two hours for the Fair's opening. His reward was this magnificent glass, though he later remarked ruefully that in spite of the fact that his friend Harald told him of it, he has not as yet offered to help pay for it! Nonetheless, A.C. will certainly share with him a glass of some truly great red wine from this famous goblet.

On one thing the group are all agreed, their collections will eventually be dispersed. The various members, and A.C. in particular, wish their collections to be on show, not only for their own enjoyment and that of their families and friends, but also to introduce as many people as possible to the beauty of English antique drinking glass – people to whom it may be unknown. A.C. has already made his Collection accessible to many, and it is rare for a month to go by without visitors being given a tour of it. The fascination and curiosity with which they view each piece is a source of amazement and delight to their host. A.C. intends to break the rule that his Collection will return to the market in only three instances, where the purchases were in a considerable measure, sentimental. First was when Neil Willcox, who has supplied most of the Collection's bottles, found two significant examples, one bearing the seal 'AC' and the other with 'I. HUBBARD'. These bottles were quite ordinary, of small value to anyone else, but obviously A.C. had to have them. Second comes a group of Bacchus glasses, exemplifying the pleasure to be had from the grape, a matter so dear to A.C.'s heart. He seldom rejects a glass with bacchic decoration. The last is something much more impressive – and even more personal – a Beilby decorated wine glass showing a sportsman, flighting duck, a dog at his side. In 1995, A.C. travelled to London to attend the auction at which this was to be sold. Sadly, the trip was made even more memorable since his father was dying at the time, and A.C. had to return immediately after the sale – having of course succeeded in buying the glass. Poignancy was added by A.C.'s fond recollections of early mornings spent in a duck blind with his father, a true and generous sportsman who always swore that it was A.C.'s shot (his very first) that dropped a green-winged teal into the water. Since his father, a crack shot, also fired, A.C. has always modestly doubted the tale. The shooting tradition extends to the next generation and A.C. and his son Crawford have had some memorable times shooting geese and duck for the Thanksgiving and Christmas tables. All the Hubbards shoot from the left shoulder, and an added attraction of the Beilby glass was A.C.'s erroneous belief that the hunter depicted there also did so. It was only quite recently pointed out to him that the Beilby hunter was actually right-shouldered. Nonetheless, A.C. has no regrets, since – as he says – he made the right decision, even if it was for the wrong reason. The purchase had another fortunate result in that after the sale, Tim Osborne of Delomosne, who had been the under-bidder, introduced himself and congratulated A.C. on acquiring such a wonderful glass. A.C. explained to Tim the added reasons for his determination to own it. Thus commenced another of A.C.'s many glass-related friendships – added to the acquisition of a sentimental piece which will one day be Crawford Hubbard's, to keep or not as he will.

# A TASTE FOR BALUSTERS

Heavy balusters can be an acquired taste. For the first five years during which he was collecting, their virtues of form, style and grace were lost on A.C. Then gradually, out of his love for early American furniture, their attraction grew on him as he came to realise how well their composition related stylistically to their era, and how superbly they fitted into the William and Mary and Pilgrim periods of interior design. The variety of form of heavy balusters is currently well represented in A.C.'s Collection, with thirty or more superb examples to show most known stem and bowl shapes and designs, as well as some outstanding rarities.

**Plate 5** *Three early balusters, probably of late seventeenth century date. Left: a pointed round funnel bowl with teared base, set on a teared cushion knop over a collar and a small, teared true baluster; folded foot. 5¹/₄ins. Centre: slightly flared round funnel bowl over stem formed of true and inverted baluster knops with wide collar between; the foot domed and folded. 6¹/₈ins. Right: a slightly smaller glass with a round funnel bowl and a stem similar to the above, again placed on a domed and folded foot. 5¹/₈ins.*

# AN APPRECIATION OF BALUSTERS

## *by Dwight P. Lanmon*

Nearly forty years ago, I began collecting eighteenth century English drinking glasses. One of the types that I coveted but could not find within my price range was a 'heavy baluster' wine glass. Made in England from the late 1690s to the 1720s, this type of glass features stems that emulate the furniture of this period. The simple, pure forms of these glasses have made them longtime favorites of collectors, indeed, many consider them to be *the* masterpieces of English glassmaking.

As noted in the introduction, heavy balusters were made of lead glass, a new formula that was perfected in London in 1676. It quickly became the standard English formula for refined table glass and, by the late 1680s, was being produced in several glasshouses. The addition of lead oxide to glass does several things: it gives the molten glass a runny quality, it enhances its brilliance (by increasing the index of refraction), it produces a heavier piece, and the bowls of drinking glasses made from it ring like bells.

The runny quality of the molten glass means that intricate, elaborate decorations are difficult to create. Softly contoured, fluid forms are easy to produce however. English glassmakers who initially began working with this new material must have been frustrated by its fluidity, for high fashion glasses made in the Venetian style were often elaborately formed and decorated. They tried making similar forms, but their attempts seemed heavy-handed by comparison. Gradually, a simplified style that took advantage of the fluidity was perfected, and by the late 1690s it had become fashionable. The new style featured stems with large, massive, turned knops, often containing intentional air bubbles that enhanced the brilliance of the glass. The knops ranged from balusters and balls to acorns, mushrooms, cylinders, and other shapes, and several forms were often combined. Examples are shown in this book.

These glasses are nearly three hundred years old, but they remain very attractive to people today. Why? Perhaps one reason is the influence of modern design on our 'taste'. Simplified, streamlined shapes are often considered to be 'successful'. This is especially true of drinking glasses. The popularity of the clean lines of 'Swedish modern' design in glass and the uncluttered look and feel of wine glasses made by Riedel, Steuben, Baccarat, and others undoubtedly contribute to that point of view. I confess to being one of those who delights in using an undecorated, colorless glass of proper shape and size to enjoy the clarity and finesse of a fine wine.

I also share the widespread opinion of collectors that a perfect union of form, decoration, and material was achieved in many early eighteenth century baluster glasses. The proportion of the bowl (diameter, height and form), stem (height, mass, size, and form), and foot (diameter and height) is usually a symphony of balance. To be sure, we sometimes overlook the fact that not all designs and workmanship in eighteenth century England were exquisite. But, when the knop is the right size for the stem and the bowl, the foot is neither too big nor too small, and the weight of the glass is neither too heavy nor too light, a baluster glass can be a delight – to view, to hold, and to drink from. In these objects, the glass itself (called the 'metal' by glassmakers), is not entirely colorless. There are usually faint, but occasionally quite noticeable, tints to the glass. Light green, blue, and blue-gray (a 'quinine' tint) are among the most common, but these tints often seem to give life to the glass. Because of the sterile purity of modern 'metal', copies of balusters seem to lack the soul of early examples.

When you look at the baluster glasses illustrated in this book, keep several words in your mind, and see how well they describe what you see. Some of the words that I think apply are *balance, strength, clarity* (form and material), and *elegance.*

Of all the knop forms that were perfected in the 1700s, my personal favourite is the acorn. I think that a perfectly formed acorn knop is very satisfying. In candlelight (the way these glasses were made to be seen and used), the lead glass shines brightly. The cap of the acorn captures more light than the nut and gives it a soft brilliance – almost like the contrast between the light cap and the darker nut of a real acorn. In most cases, there is a small, intentional air bubble in the cap, which increases its brilliance. The fingers can get a good grip on the stem so that it does not slip. The base of the bowl, which often has an air bubble, also captures and refracts the light. There is a comfortable weight to the glass, and, when the bowl is filled with wine, it is not top-heavy.

What makes me admire a certain baluster glass, but not

another? There are many factors. Rarity of the form of the knop is high on the list. Acorns and mushrooms are more sought after than ball or angular knops or inverted balusters (rounded, tapered knops, imitating architectural balusters, with the heavy part at the top). They are preferred because they are rarer. Glasses with wonderful cylinder knops are just as desirable as acorns because they are very rare as well. Rarity is not the only factor that counts for me, however.

The second factor, in my opinion, is the success of the form, in other words, is the glass well 'put together'? I actually prefer a well-proportioned glass with a common stem form to one that has a rare knop but is not constructed as gracefully. Many collectors certainly don't agree with me. For example, ovoid-shaped 'egg' knops are among the rarest of all baluster knops, and consequently are avidly sought. However, I have never seen an 'egg'

they are not very convincing, lacking, as they generally do, any tint or 'personality'. In early glasses, some accidental bubbles are to be expected, but large ones or too many can disfigure the clarity of a bowl. Heavy striations in the glass can also disfigure it. For me, the quality of the 'metal' strongly affects the value of a glass.

Fourth, I evaluate condition. Chipped feet are rare on baluster glasses because the foot rims are usually folded, that is, they were doubled back to make them stronger. Chipped bowls are more common, and scratches in the bowl are the most frequent defect. These may be caused by injudicious and over-enthusiastic attempts to clean the clouding that sometimes afflicts lead glass. Since it is comparatively soft, abrasive substances may damage it. Clouding need not be a worry since it can be expertly removed without the use of chemicals. Defects must be evaluated on a case-by-case basis. Some chips can be

**Fig. 23** *This rare 1715 invoice shows glasses (balusters?) sold by weight. I cannot think that this was standard practice. Glass was taxed by weight, certainly, but I believe that this tax was levied on the raw material, not the finished product.*                    W.L.

baluster that I thought was successful, so I have never considered acquiring one. Also, the bowls on some glasses do not seem very graceful – and that can diminish my appreciation of a glass, no matter what the knop is.

The third factor is the quality of the metal. Is it brilliant, or does it lack luster and shine? Does it have a hint of bluish, grayish, or greenish tint, and is that tint too strong? Fortunately, fakes are not much of a problem with 'baluster' glasses. Some imitations have been made, but

repaired so that they become almost invisible and shallow scratches can be remove by polishing. Feet or bowls that have been trimmed to remove chips can be devastating to the appearance of a glass, because the removal of material changes the proportion of the parts. However, if the glass is rare enough or beautiful enough, a serious defect may be overlooked.

One personal experience might demonstrate what I mean. I was once delighted to be offered a magnificent baluster ale glass with an acorn knop. To my knowledge, only three were known. One, in perfect condition, is in the collection of The Corning Museum of Glass, and I admire it immensely. Another example was illustrated in an early auction catalogue, I do not know where it is today. The ale glass that was offered to me is an extremely rare form, it has a brilliant acorn knop, and the proportion of bowl to stem to foot is perfect. However, it has a significant flaw: its foot had been broken and replaced. The new foot had been removed from another broken glass, but it is of the correct form, size, and color. The repair was done so well that unless the glass is examined carefully with a magnifying glass, it is undetectable. I considered for a moment whether I should wait until a third perfect one showed up, but I quickly decided that I would prefer to enjoy the glass now, and so I bought it. I knew that, if another undamaged example were ever offered to me, I could then decide whether to replace it or not. In the meantime, this glass remains one of my favorites, and the fact that is repaired never crosses my mind when I see it.

The difference between a fine glass and a lesser example of similar construction is usually discernable to an advanced collector, but not necessarily to a beginner. Soon, however, a collector should see that many quite ordinary eighteenth century glasses are pleasing to the eye and touch. In addition, as I have noted, the rarest glass may not have the personal appeal that a commoner one has. So, there is wide room for finding, owning, and enjoying glasses that are nearly three hundred years old, that represent a golden age of glassmaking, and that are examples of a high – for me, the very highest – point of design for the material: lead glass.

**Plate 6**, *page 34. A rare baluster ale glass from the Collection. 7³/₄ins. (Formerly in the Walter Smith Collection).*

26

# THE DISCONTENTED MR. GREEN

Before proceeding to balusters proper, a slightly earlier drinking glass style warrants mention. Although almost all the glass in A.C.'s Collection is English in origin, an occasional piece is present because of its strong English associations. Such a glass is illustrated on the left of plate 7. This type was imported from Venice by the Glass Sellers Company in the 1660s and 1670s. John Greene, a founder and later Master of the Company, sent endless drawings (frequently super-imposed on each other, presumably to save paper) to Alessio Morelli in Venice, together with a string of barely legible complaints about breakage and cost. In spite of his constant exhortations to "...make them stout... for tavern use" few have survived. This fact, as well as Greene's letters, make it clear that glassware at the time was not solely the prerogative of the well-to-do, but was also found in public places. However, the taverns of the day where glass might be in use, were a cut above the more commonplace inns which would have served their drinks in pewter or leather vessels – likelier to survive than glass. Of course, the private house and the really superior establishment might well use silver.

Certainly, Greene's dissatisfaction with Morelli's glass resulted in the improvement and enlargement of the native glass industry. English glass of the later seventeenth century, though still strongly Venetian influenced (like the glass on the right of the illustration), was developing a character entirely of its own, eventually leading – via George Ravenscroft's mould decorated lead glass – to the great (and unique) tradition of the English heavy baluster. Prior to this period (and probably overlapping it), some elegant pieces were produced in the Dutch *façon-de-Venise* style, often with gadrooning in imitation of contemporary silver or the 'nipt diamond waies' decoration used and described by Ravenscroft, plate 8. Two late seventeenth century transitional *façon-de-Venise* wine glasses, plates 11 and 12, page 29, in A.C.'s Collection foreshadow the styles of the early eighteenth century, one in greenish, the other in greyish lead glass. The mead glass has diamond moulded base to the bowl, and the wine glass has heavy double-gathered gadrooning. Many glasses of this period have a certain fluid look to the metal.

A very interesting transitional glass is shown here, plate 9, page 28. Though crafted in full lead glass, it is still Venetian in style (note the Greene-like funnel bowl and narrowly folded foot), but beginning to take on baluster characteristics. The fine stipple engraving is Dutch of a much later date, in the manner of the master engraver Hoolart. Now in A.C.'s hands, the glass once formed part of the renowned Guepin Collection.

**Plate 7** *Heights 6¼ins and 6⅝ins.*

**Plate 8** *Heights 5¾ins and 5½ins.*

*Plate 9*, page 27.
Height 5¹/₂ins.

**Plate 10**, *page 27.*

## GIANTS AMONG THE GREAT

Compared to glasses of later date, balusters often seem to be big. Sometimes they are gigantic. A standard-sized bottle of about the same date as these two, plate 20, page 32, 11ins, gives an idea of their capacity. The full size octagonal decanter jug, plate 21, page 32, could barely fill the baluster of equal height that stands beside it.

For really monumental proportions, plate 14, page 30, how about this splendid example of the glassmaker's skill in manipulating large mass into subtle shape? A magnificently proportioned vessel though it undoubtedly is, its most striking feature remains its vast capacity – no less than four bottles. A standard sized goblet from the same 'chair', and a rare, tiny glass (as small in capacity as a modern liqueur glass) stand next to it. Note this group, plate 13, opposite, where a superb, huge acorn knopped baluster dwarfs a rare candlestick (8⁵/₈ins), and another earlier acorn knopped baluster of more usual size.

## SOME VARIANTS OF SIZE AND SHAPE

A plain stemmed, pan-topped cordial, plate 18, page 31, of a slightly later period, 6¹/₂ins, stands beside an unusually heavily knopped cordial of about 1720.

Another giant stands by its smaller contemporary, plate 19, page 31 – fine, early glasses both, circa 1700-1710, respectively 11¹/₈ins and 4⁷/₈ins in height.

An elegant drawn trumpet over a drop knop and a domed foot, plate 15, page 31, which is – unusually – not folded.

Two early baluster drams, plates 16 and 17, page 31. Plate 17 with an annular knopped and domed foot. Plate 16, also shown filled with wine, is an example of the deceptive-bowled or 'toastmaster's' glass, containing far less liquid than it appears to hold, thus facilitating the drinking of multiple toasts while still remaining upright.

Early eighteenth century glasses with moulded pedestal stems, plates 121 and 123, page 90, often referred to as 'Silesian'. That on the left has a rare ribbed bowl and foot, the other has a four-sided stem, moulded with crowns on the shoulders and diamonds on top of the sides. Both are 6ins high (I shall return to this very special glass when talking about commemoratives, page 90). Both glasses date from about the time of George I's coronation (1714).

The range of bowl styles is well represented throughout the Hubbard Collection, from those of the complex-knopped glasses, plate 19, page 31, with their elegant, solid-based round funnels, the very rare straight-

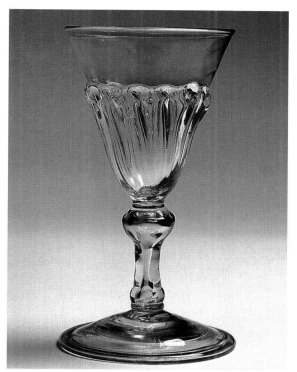

**Plate 11**, *page 27. Height 6¹/₄ins.*

**Plate 12**, *page 27. Height 5¹/₂ins.*

**Plate 13**, *page 28. A giant acorn knopped baluster; a baluster candlestick, 8⁵/₈ins, and another earlier acorn knopped baluster, 6¹/₂ins.*

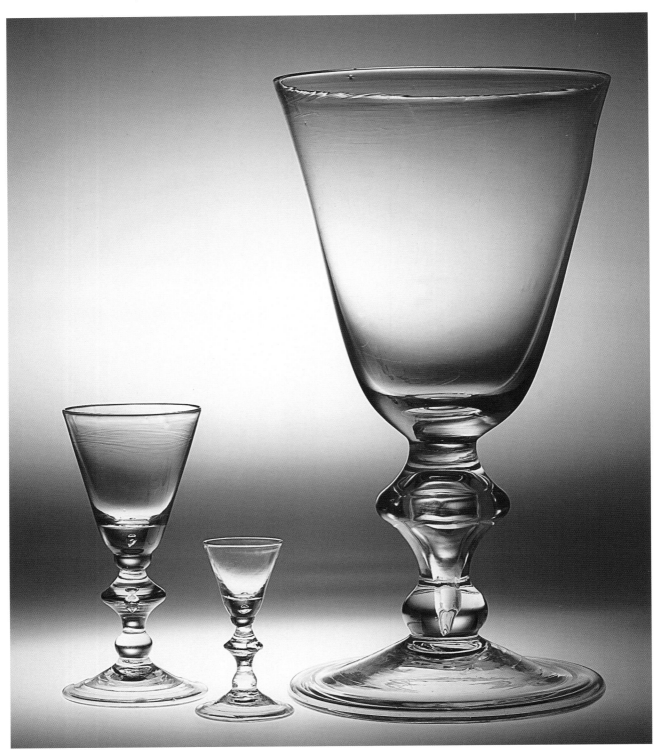

**Plate 14**, *page 28.  Heights 6³/₄ins, 3⁷/₈ins and 14¹/₂ins.*

**Plate 17**, *page 28.*
*Height 4⁷/₈ins.*

**Plate 16**, *page 28.*
*Height 4¹/₄ins.*

**Plate 15**, *page 28.  Height 6³/₄ins.*

**Plate 18**, *page 28.  Height 7ins and 6¹/₂ins.*

**Plate 19**, *page 28.  Height 4⁷/₈ins and 11¹/₈ins.*

**Plate 20**, *page 28. Heights 10¹/₂ins and 11ins .*

**Plate 21**, *page 28. Heights both 8³/₄ins.*

**Plate 23**, *page 34. Heights 5³/₄ins and 5¹/₂ins.*

**Plate 22**, *page 34.*

**Plate 24**, *page 34. Heights 5⁵/₈ins - 6³/₄ins.*

sided ale glass – plate 6, page 26 – to the elongated bells – also rarities – of plate 28, page 36.

The shapes of the three smaller glasses, plate 24, page 33, are more difficult to describe, the stems are drop knops and the bowls approximate to double ogees. They date from the late seventeenth century and are developed from imported Venetian models. Plate 26, page 36 is a very early example of a drop knop which has an elongated tulip bowl, suggesting a seventeenth century date.

The heavier true baluster illustrated here, plate 23, page 33, with the cylinder stemmed glass, is a finely balanced bell-bowled example.

Two further splendidly knopped balusters, plates 27 and 30, pages 36 and 37 show the normal round funnel bowl containing a tear, as it so often does. Note the unusually high domed foot of plate 27.

Since weight was not a consideration (the 'metal' was cheap and as yet untaxed), the feet of early balusters were usually folded and quite often also domed. This is clearly seen in the double drop knopped, bell bowled glasses illustrated opposite, plate 25.

## THE RARER KNOPS AND BOWLS

A splendid 'egg' stem like the specimen illustrated, plate 31, page 37 displays this style of knopping to perfection. One of the very rarest types, it is strange that it was not more frequently used.

Almost equally unusual is the large mushroom knop, plates 29 and 32, page 37, with its heavy based thistle bowl.

The bowls of many of the best baluster glasses are elegant round funnels – possibly the most satisfying shape. Plates 30, 31 and 33, page 37 show good examples on rare stems; egg, cushion and air bead.

## GLASSMAKING MADE EASY
## BALUSTROIDS AND PLAIN STEMS
### (Increased Demand Demands Simpler Forms)

The baluster period was followed, in the interests of weight reduction (because of taxation), by ever-shrinking knop size in the stems of wine glasses, eventually leading to their complete disappearance, with the striking exception of Newcastles. Folding of the foot was to remain for some time. It is a shame that it was not retained (except in a very few examples) for the 'cotton twist' – the main glass of the later eighteenth century – since the device hugely strengthens the edge of the foot

and largely prevents the ugly chipping to which unfolded feet are prone. It must be said that some knopping on balustroid glasses became so rudimentary that one wonders why the gaffer bothered to form it at all. Eventually of course he didn't, and simple glasses with plain stems were produced in vast quantities. The commonest form was the drawn trumpet, a glass simply made of two pieces, the stem (usually having an inset tear for decorative effect) from which the bowl was manipulated into a trumpet shape, and a foot which was normally folded. These glasses were so common even in this century that Mrs. Graydon Stannus (of 'Graystan' glass fame), who operated a glasshouse and cutting-shop in Chelsea, London, in the 1920s, bought large quantities of them which she 'improved' by having them cut with shallow 'Irish style' slices. Such glasses still appear on the market, variously described. Other small-bowled glasses were made in three pieces, the bowl usually following its balustroid predecessors in being either an ogee, a bell or a round funnel. Again, at least among the earlier ones, the foot was folded.

As to decoration, the most famous are the trumpet bowls inscribed in diamond-point with the Jacobite anthem – the so called 'Amen' glasses. It is unwise to accept any of these other than the few which have a firm provenance dating back to Jacobite times. However, some of the best and most believable Jacobite engraving is also found on drawn trumpet glasses, executed with the wheel, not the diamond-point.

## SHORT-LIVED SIMPLE FORMS
## INCISED TWISTS AND HOLLOW STEMS

A stem which enjoyed a brief vogue contemporaneously with early air twists was the incised twist. At first glance, these can be taken for multi-spiral air twists, but touch and inspection reveal that the decoration is external, consisting of finely incised lines which have been twisted into a spiral. The stems are sometimes very finely and carefully made, like the perry glass on page 91, but can also be coarse and unevenly twisted. Goblets as well as wine glasses are found, but the fashion was short-lived.

Another form of stem which never really caught on was the hollow cylinder. More than just an elongated tear, this stem was formed separately from bowl and foot. The only point to making this seems to have been lightness, and quality glasses with this stem are again not very common.

**Plate 25**  *Heights 7¹/₈ins and 6⁵/₈ins.*

**Plate 26**, *page 34.  Height 5¹/₂ins.*

**Plate 27**, *page 34.  Height 7¹/₂ins.*

**Plate 28**, *page 34.  Height 7¹/₂ins.*

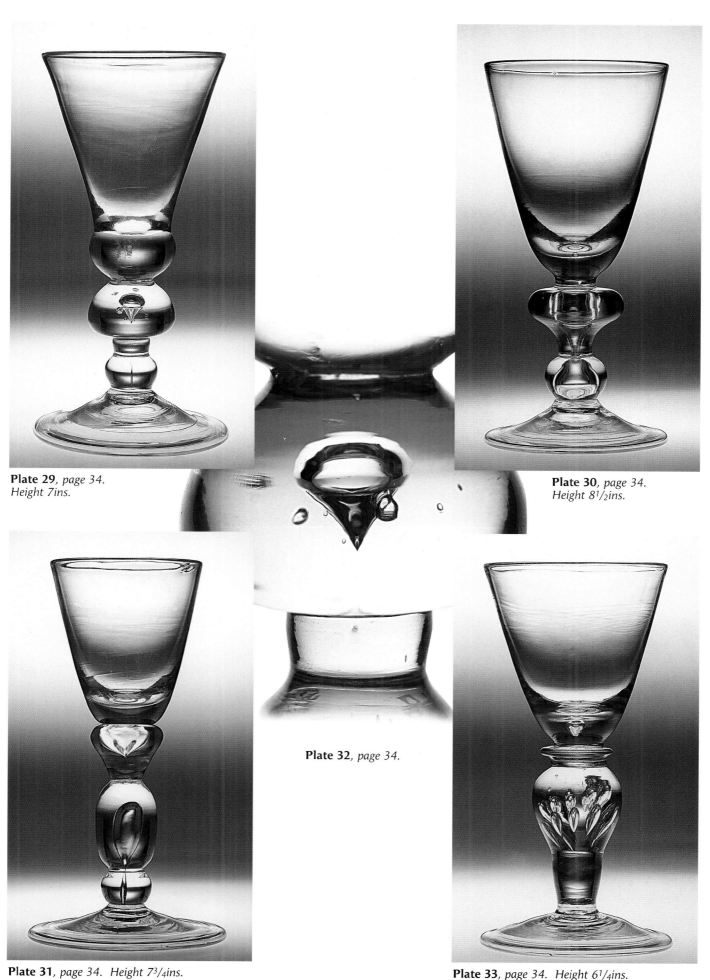

**Plate 29**, *page 34.*
*Height 7ins.*

**Plate 30**, *page 34.*
*Height 8¹/₂ins.*

**Plate 32**, *page 34.*

**Plate 31**, *page 34. Height 7³/₄ins.*

**Plate 33**, *page 34. Height 6¹/₄ins.*

# NEWCASTLES – NEW SKILLS

Many collectors will consider the light balusters produced by the Newcastle glasshouses to be, in both design and execution, the finest of English drinking glasses. Their teared, knopped stems can be extraordinarily graceful, and their capacious (by Georgian standards) bowls are often elegantly proportioned – especially those which follow the round funnel tradition. The other frequently encountered shape – the bell – is not always so successful. Strangely, few other bowl types are found – the plain funnel, the slightly flared lip, are exceptions that spring to mind. Whatever the shape, few of the bowls were left undecorated. Vast numbers were shipped to the Low Countries, where virtually all were engraved for an eager Dutch market – sometimes by major artists of great technique and amazing skill, working with both wheel and diamond-point – while many were unfortunately spoilt by less skilled artisans. It should always be borne in mind by the would-be collector in any field that not everything made in the past was splendid and worth collecting. Georgian craftsmen, too, could produce meretricious work, and age alone does not beautify. It is a mystery to me as to why so few lovely Newcastle glasses were left unadorned. Even the great Beilbys could not resist enamelling some of them, when they could have found vehicles more in need of their exquisite talents. I do not, of course, imply that the work of the Beilbys in any way detracted from the Newcastles that they decided (perhaps on commission) to decorate. I simply state my opinion that the best glasses of Newcastle design are well able to stand on their own.

One reason why Dutch engravers preferred them to any other type of European glass is because the high lead content of the English glass rendered it softer and easier to work. Myriad motifs were applied to their bowls, often as unique gifts or love tokens, frequently also armorials or commemoratives, political and poetic allusions and others whose meanings, personal or otherwise, are totally lost or can merely be guessed at or are clouded by conjecture.

The sum of this is that it is not common to find plain Newcastles – some even had their stems and feet faceted almost certainly at a later date. Therefore the magnificent examples in the Collection will chiefly be found amongst the special pieces which, although splendid in their own right, also superbly display the very finest painted or engraved decoration.

That said, I have an interesting tale to tell – one for which I have so far been unable to find an explanation. Many years ago, I purchased a multi-volume late eighteenth century edition of the Encyclopaedia Britannica (1795 I think it was). It turned out to be incomplete and I was glad to get rid of it. However, I very much regret that I did not keep the section on glass, which ran to many pages and included a large number of chemical formulae, furnace temperatures and general advice on its manufacture. The history of the industry in England was covered and there

**Plate 34** *Height 7³/₈ins.*

was considerable information on the various glasshouses in England and Ireland. But viewed in the light of what we have been taught today, it contained some very curious statements. For example, it said that the principle production of the Bristol and Nailsea houses was coloured glass, almost always red! So much, one might think, for the famous 'Bristol blue'! But is the statement true? For as far as we can ascertain today, eighteenth century English red glass is virtually unknown. Then came the real blow to our preconceptions: the Encyclopaedia stated that the output of Newcastle was very large, usually coloured and easily recognisable by its mass produced, inferior quality, quite unsuited to use outside of inns and taverns! However this idea arose, it has to be false, since there is plenty of documentary and pictorial evidence showing these highly refined glasses in use – those that we think of as Newcastles today.

It seems appropriate here to show an exquisitely engraved Newcastle, plate 35, of typical form, which not only has been worked by a master hand but is also the subject of an amusing anecdote. The engraving is an allegory of 'liberty', a matter much on eighteenth century Dutch minds, as well as those of the French. Alan Milford tells the story of its discovery:

'A dealer traversing the Nieuwe Spiegelstraat in Amsterdam was offering this glass to the specialist glass dealers, all of whom considered the subject insufficiently unusual for the price asked. Having failed here, the owner proceeded down the road to the Spiegelgracht. The asking price had dropped by then and it was purchased by a general dealer, Barendt Groen (now sadly deceased), who liked it and told one of his collectors to come and have a look. The collector bought it, and later in the evening rang up to ask, "Did you know that this glass was signed?"

"No," says Berry, "What's the signature?"

"J.Sang fecit Amsterdam 1757", came the answer.

"Oh, really? How much do you want for it?"

A deal was struck, the glass re-purchased, and I was immediately summoned, since it was known that I was looking for just such a glass for Clive Quie. The signature, plate 36, had gone unnoticed as it is very finely engraved underneath the foot rim and looks at first glance like wear.

Incidentally, when Clive's collection was later put in store pending the settlement of his will, the auction expert preparing the inventory of the glasses also missed the signature. This shows that there is always the possibility of some treasure that needs discovering lurking in even the most exalted places. The glass has now found its destined niche in the Collection'.

Other splendid Newcastles engraved by Dutch masters are to be found elsewhere in this book, glasses such as plate 34 engraved for the merchantman 'Cornelia and Theodora', and rarities like those executed for the great Dutch East India Company about which more will be said later.

**Plate 35** *Height 7ins.*

**Plate 36**

# GREAT QUANTITY FROM SMALL MEASURE – SOME SPECULATIONS ON GEORGIAN DRINKING HABITS

The exceedingly small bowl size of the majority of post-baluster period eighteenth century wine glasses is a feature which I have never heard satisfactorily explained. There is an obvious reason for limiting the capacity of so-called 'toastmaster' or deceptive bowls (that less alcohol was being consumed than was apparent – a necessity for the proposer of multiple toasts). And while accepting that ratafia or 'surfeit water' was so powerfully alcoholic that it required an elongated thimble of a bowl to reduce evaporation and promote elegant sipping, that long-stemmed, tiny-bowled cordial glasses, sometimes referred to as 'tea-tray glasses', were appropriate vessels from which fashionable ladies could elegantly consume strong liqueurs, that crude gin glasses held precisely a hap'orth (or perhaps a farthing's worth), of gin when brim full*, that, in short, many bowl types were designed with a purpose in mind – why then the limited (and uneven) capacity of the usual so-called 'wine glass' bowl? Or for that matter the bowls of ale and cider glasses? Especially when we are aware of the vast strong beverage consumption of most of our forefathers, why didn't more of them use the much rarer goblet-bowled glasses – certainly available to them and more in line in capacity with drinking vessels in use on the continent? It can scarcely have been for reasons of economy – a virtue not much practised in those days. No, for some reason the English Georgian gentleman preferred to take his wine, fortified or not, his ale, his cider, from a small-bowled glass. He could still drink his six or eight bottles, but he took them a little at a time, and having much leisure over a long daily period, starting with sherry for breakfast and ending, if he was still conscious, with brandy nightcaps. Needless to add, such a regime coupled as it was with a carnivorous, high fat diet, frequently resulted in agonising attacks of gout, and early death.

Pictorial evidence and the existence of many of those curious lipped bowls called 'wine-glass rinsers', still in occasional use in Edwardian times, indicate to us that no elaborate table-setting of various glasses suitable for the consumption of diverse wines was usual even at very formal Georgian meals. Rather, the same glass was repeatedly rinsed as the wines were changed, as indeed were the mouths of the diners of the period, who used that other individual piece of table glass, the tumbler, which was found on the tables of the rich.

**Plate 37** *Heights 6⁷/₈ins - 7³/₄ins.*

Between courses, this small water-filled hemispherical bowl was used to cleanse the palate. The water, I fear, not being drunk but returned from mouth to bowl. Georgian table manners were not for the queasy modern stomach.

It is strange that no examples exist of any designs that we would now consider appropriate for the savouring of fine wines – no incurving of the bowl to capture bouquet, nor, until the nineteenth century, the elongated bowls that are today considered best suited to champagne and other sparkling wines. 'Champagnes' are specified on the invoice, page 43, but we do not know their shape.

*Remember the tavern advertising slogan of the day: 'DRUNK FOR A PENNY, DEAD DRUNK FOR TUPPENCE, STRAW FREE'.

## RATAFIAS –
## AN EXAMPLE OF TINY BOWL SIZE

A.C. stumbled on ratafia – the drink that is – in the city of Reims, during a tasting tour he was on in the Champagne region. He had found the very narrow cylindrical flute glasses used to serve it to be highly attractive in form, but – like everyone encountering them for the first time – had speculated on what style of very strong liquor their tiny capacity bowls were designed to hold. Knowing what the glasses were called, he was delighted to come across some small bottles of ratafia in a Reims wine store. Naturally, he bought several. When next exhibiting at the Hunt Valley Antiques Show, Tony Werneke came by to view A.C.'s Collection. He and A.C. both sampled the beverage from the appropriate glasses. Their comments are not favourable! Some ratafias are illustrated, plate 37; opaque twist stems are the most usual, but a rare one on the left has an air twist stem.

## AT A TWIST OF THE BREATH

On looking at an air twist stem, especially one that shines as brightly as entrapped silver, should I be in romantic mood, it may occur to me that captured within its little sparkling tubes is preserved the very air breathed centuries ago by the skilled artisan who created it. The artifice wonderfully enlivens the glass from within, an effect that must have originally been noticed in the tears contained in baluster and plain-stemmed glasses – probably initially deriving from bubbles accidentally introduced in the manufacturing process. Since teared knops preceded air twists, it also seems likely that accidental twisting of the tears in these suggested the deliberate creation of this decorative effect.

Whatever its origins (and it seems to have been an exclusively English idea) many versions of the design were successfully used throughout the mid section and early second half of the eighteenth century. Indeed, it overlapped the introduction of white enamel and colour twist stems, and was on rare occasions even incorporated with them in the so-called 'mixed twists', a fine example of which we see here on the left of plate 53, page 48, with a delicate little cordial bowl. With composite stems, as shown in plates 38 and 39, page 42, the baluster tradition still persists, especially in the heavy, teared knop of the larger glass, plate 38. Note, too, the very characteristic fruiting vine engraving. On each glass the multi-spiral section above the foot and knops is formed in one piece with the bowl.

Another instance of an air twist harking back to earlier form is plate 43, page 44, showing as it does a multi-spiral stem of inverted baluster shape, and a most unusual, double gathered ale bowl, spirally moulded over two thirds of its height – a rare transitional feature that harks back to the seventeenth century.

The commonest air twist is of drawn trumpet shape, the stem containing many elongated and twisted air-bubbles, but following in outline the design of its plain-stemmed predecessors. This glass is made in only two pieces and as noted the air bubbles probably arose fortuitously, and were subsequently both multiplied and manipulated into shape by twisting. All sorts of variants followed, with many complex elaborations of the twist. A lovely example is the shining spiral stem of the cordial, plate 42, page 44, so bright that the type is sometimes called a 'mercury' twist. It adds great sparkling attraction to the glass. Additionally, and most unusually, the bowl is engraved with red currants, presumably for the eponymous cordial. The shoulder knop of the other glass gives interest to an otherwise conventional stem. The bowl is also somewhat different, in that it replaces the commoner round funnel type.

A curiosity seen here, plate 46, page 45, is a so-called captain glass. These towering pieces, although very rare, are well documented. They seem always to have cotton twist stems and usually a terraced firing foot – suggesting that they were perhaps the prerogative of a club chairman who could use it to rap the table to call for order, their very height lending authority to his position. The single series, knopped enamel twist glass placed beside the captain glass is interesting for its unusual construction – the bowl is so skillfully joined to the stem that the glass appears to be made in only two pieces.

Successful knopping of air twist stems required great skill, in order not to cause distortion of the twist. Two knops are usually as much as was attempted and any further knopping becomes increasingly rare, and not always successful, in direct proportion to the number of knops created. Picture then the rarity of the two five-knopped stems illustrated here, plate 40, page 44, which must have taxed the skill of even the most experienced gaffer.

Although the multi-spiral predominated for some time, considerable variety also came into being – cables, 'mercury' and double-series twists of varying complexity. By the mid eighteenth century, bowl size had, in general, become rather small, see comments on page 40, but there were exceptions, plate 41, page 44, as this

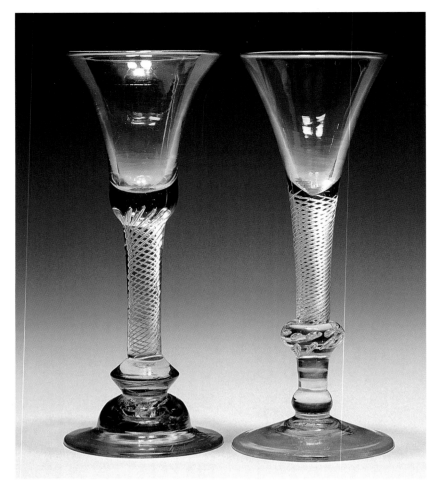

**Plate 39**, *page 41. Heights both 6³/₄ins.*

**Plate 38**, *pages 41 and 46. Height 9ins.*

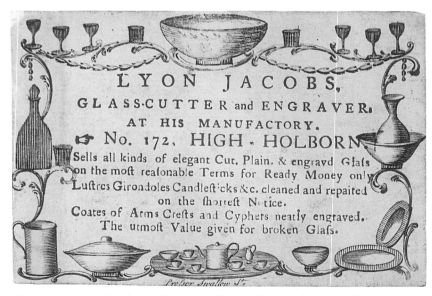

**Fig. 24** *Lyon Jacobs, glass and pottery seller, could clearly be counted on to engrave anything on glass that was asked of him. The vessels he sold for this purpose seem to be of simpler shape – therefore presumably less expensive – than any you will find in the Collection. Social climbers need only supply Jacobs with an armorial device of their own design, hopefully thus improving both their glass and their social standing. Note the offer to buy broken glass, called cullet, which could be re-used by adding it carefully and in small quantities to a pot of molten glass, injudicious haste or over-great quantity could cause bubbles to form in the 'metal'. © Copyright The British Museum.*

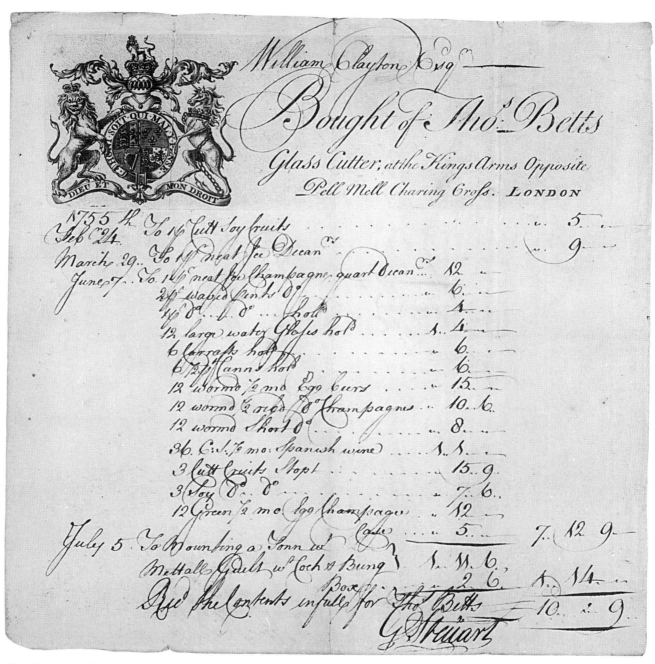

**Fig. 25** *From this glass sellers invoice dated 1755, it would seem probable that the 'wormd' glasses of Thos. Betts were air twists – though since Betts was a large and fashionable retailer, they might well be the (at that time) 'new fangled' white enamel twists. Water glasses (which may be either tumblers or the mouth rinsers to which I have referred) seem expensive, carafes cheap. What did the twelve green champagne glasses look like? And likewise the quart decanter for champagne? William Clayton, as befitted a Georgian gentleman, used enormous quantities of glassware, but (typically) was in no hurry about paying his bills! © Copyright The British Museum.*

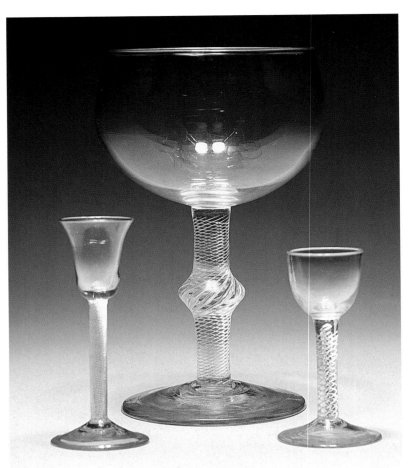

**Plate 40**, *page 41.  Heights both 6⁷/₈ins.*

**Plate 41**, *page 41.  Heights 5ins, 8³/₄ins and 4¹/₄ins.*

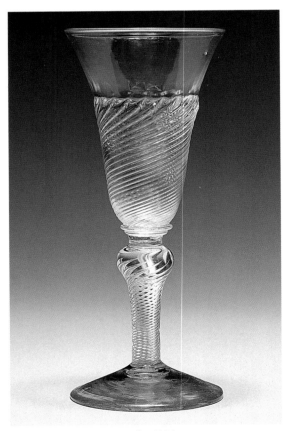

**Plate 42**, *page 41.  Heights 7ins and 6¹/₂ins.*

**Plate 43**, *page 41.  Height 6¹/₂ins.*

**Plate 45**, *page 46.*
*Height 5³/₄ins.*

**Plate 44**, *page 46. Heights 7¹/₄ins and 8ins.*

**Plate 46**, *page 41. Heights 6¹/₂ins and 10ins.*

**Plate 47**, *page 46. Heights 6⁷/₈ins and 4³/₄ins.*

illustration shows. The little glasses are tiny, but the large one holds a quart! Stem differences will also be noted.

By the 1760s, the designs of air twists had grown very refined. The style coincided with the development of fashionable enamel twists, and reached its zenith with glasses like this pan-topped, centre knopped example, plate 45, page 45. This acme of air twist elegance went on to be copied in white enamel and even colour twist stems.

Various decorative devices were used to embellish, with wheel engraving the bowls of both air and enamel twists, most commonly fruiting vine on wine glasses and hop and barley on ales, plates 38 and 44, pages 42 and 45.

Moulding and cutting also occurs, plates 47 and 52, pages 45 and 48, and occasionally something truly remarkable, like the diamond moulding on the double series opaque twist goblet and glass in plate 54, page 48.

Height and bowl shape seem to have been arbitrary matters, so that a tiny cordial bowl could sit on a stem of any length, plate 55, page 48. As noted, there was considerable overlap between air and enamel designs – earlier, simpler white twists often merely copying their airy predecessors. But as the style caught on, much greater complications were attempted – feats of glassmanship which would have been impossible using air alone. White enamel rods of a wide variety of patterns were drawn and twisted, singly or in combinations of up to three, into the most elaborate of stem forms, until the only possibility of further internal change became the colouring of the enamels, a technique which we will look at presently.

The pretty, elongated, narrow cylinders or trumpets of ratafia glasses could sometimes extend even higher than tall cordials, plate 48, and are usually found with white enamel twist stems. Although their elegance of design is greatly admired by him, A.C.'s views of the liquor they were made to contain are expressed elsewhere in this book, see page 41.

Many further examples of both air and enamel twist stems and bowl shapes will be found elsewhere in A.C.'s Collection – amongst the Beilbys, Lynns, commemorative and political pieces, Jacobites, and the dazzling array of colour twists.

## SEWING THREADS INTO THE STEM 'COTTON TWISTS' – MULTIPLE DESIGNS IN DRAWN ENAMEL

These glasses, with their white enamel twist stems, affectionately known by trade and collector alike as 'cotton twists', on account of the thread-like appearance of the finer spirals, were the fashionable drinking vessels of the upper classes during much of the second half of the

**Plate 48**
*Heights 5⁵/₈ins and 7¹/₂ins.*

eighteenth century. The permutations and combinations of twists used are enormous and only a really driven man would attempt to form and classify a fully representative collection based on all possible stem constructions. Many years ago Barrington Haynes (the Duveen of antique glass dealers) formulated an elaborate classification of all eighteenth century English drinking glass stems, bowl shapes and feet. This scholarly work is of course still available, but I don't believe that today's collector is greatly influenced by these somewhat esoteric considerations, but rather – rightly in my view – regards each glass on its overall merits of aesthetic proportion, elegance and so on, as one might judge the work of a painter not by details like brush strokes but by the total effect of the particular painting that is viewed.

Nonetheless, there is obviously room in any collection for examples of extreme interest that are included on rarity grounds alone, appearance regardless, since such glasses may owe their very scarcity to the fact that they were of unsuccessful design, and their production therefore suspended. Such pieces are of obvious historical interest, even when their appearance is not particularly pleasing.

Here we have mainly considered unadorned glasses with air and white enamel twist stems. Later, we will look at the adornment of both, together with that of other types – enamelling, engraving, gilding – and will also be looking at spectacularly rare forms which for one reason or another stand apart from any general grouping. In the meantime, the glasses which we show here are well worth studying for their form alone. This is legion, but there are certain groupings that can be based on shape – like cordials, ratafias, ales etc. One such group shows almost all types of stem, but many of the feet types – terraced, strung, oversewn and so on – are unique to the group. Bowl shape is usually ogee, round funnel or bell. I refer, of course, to the firing glasses. The features they have in common are small bowl capacity, rudimentary stem and heavy foot (used to rap the table in response to toasts, called 'firing'). A.C. has a good representation, plates 50 and 51. Their bowls could be deceptive, shown on the left of plate 49 (later we look at a spectacular Beilby example, enamelled TEMPERANCE) or could carry masonic or other club symbols. This one, on the right of plate 49, shows a roasting grill and comes from the

convivial 'Beefsteak Club', of which the great John Wilkes, amongst other notables of the time, was a member. He was also a member of the notorious 'Hellfire Club', from which, perhaps fortunately, no glasses are known to survive, though an exception may be some cordials crudely painted with a phallus in coloured enamels.

The experienced collector knows that the difference is slight between a good example of practically any artifact or work of art and one which merits the adjective 'superb'. It often takes a trained and cultivated eye to notice it – or an eye which is guided by visual memory. Therefore it behoves both serious student and collector to avail themselves of the chance to examine the very best specimens – a term which may accurately be applied to many of A.C.'s glasses.

**Plate 49**  *Heights 4¹/₂ins and 3⁵/₈ins.*

**Plate 50**  *Heights 4ins and 4¹/₄ins.*

**Plate 51**  *Heights 3³/₄ins, 4ins and 4¹/₄ins.*

**Plate 52**, *page 46.*
*Heights 6ins*
*and 5⁷/₈ins.*

**Plate 53**, *page 41. Heights 6ins, 6ins and 5¹/₂ins.*

**Plate 54**, *page 46. Heights 6³/₄ins and 5ins.*

**Plate 55**, *page 46. Heights 3¹/₄ins, 5¹/₂ins and 3⁵/₈ins.*

# RINGING THE CHANGES

The unique and characteristic ring decoration of so-called Lynn glassware make it instantly recognisable.

Recent research has shown that (contrary to the widely held belief) it is unlikely that this very interesting group was made in the Norfolk town of King's Lynn, since the only known glasshouse there is recorded as having been closed down in 1747, and much of the glass is plainly later than this date. But there is a great likelihood that somewhere awaiting discovery in East Anglia, lurks the remains of a glasshouse (or glasshouses) where this finely made lead crystal was produced. The metal is of consistently high quality, and the decorative tooled rings are found – widely or narrowly spaced, like ripples on a limpid pond – on vessels of all sorts. Why this design feature should have been adopted and used on

virtually every piece of glass produced, to the exclusion of all else, is a mystery, but this idiosyncratic feature adds very considerably to its charm. It occurs on everything, from the bowls of cotton twist wine glasses, shown here with an unusual air twist ale, plate 61, page 51, and three rare firing glasses, plate 58, page 50, to a double series cotton twist goblet with a folded foot, plate 59, page 50. From carafes, tumblers, tankards and fingerbowls, plate 62, page 51, to little early cream jugs, bonnet glasses and even tazzae, plate 60, page 50.

Accomplished gaffers working at this mysterious glasshouse, while always (as far as we know) preserving the eponymous ring style, could create masterpieces of simple form from early shaft-and-globe decanter to sophisticated pan-topped ale, plate 57. Although specific examples are scarce, the design range is great. An unexpected feature on enamel twist glasses of Lynn design is the folded foot, normally associated with air twist and plain stemmed glasses, but seen here on the right-hand cotton twist of plate 61, page 51 and plates 57 (below) and plate 59, page 50.

On rare occasions, Lynn glass carries decoration in addition to its rings, this mallet decanter, engraved for WHITE WINE is an extreme example, plate 56.

**Plate 56**
*Height 10¹/₂ins.*

**Plate 57**  *Heights 8¹/₂ins and 9³/₄ins.*

49

**Plate 58**, *page 49.  Heights 4¹/₈ins, 4ins and 4¹/₄ins.*

**Plate 59**, *page 49.*
*Height 7¹/₄ins.*

**Plate 60**, *page 49.  Diam. 9¹/₂ins, height 3ins, jug height 3³/₄ins.*

**Plate 61**, *page 49. Heights 5¹/₂ins - 6¹/₄ins.*

**Plate 62**, *page 49. Heights 7¹/₄ins, 3ins, 5¹/₄ins, 3³/₄ins and 7¹/₈ins.*

# COLOUR TWISTS –
# THE PINNACLE OF THE ART

Colour twists are the splendid eventual refinement of the introduction of enamel into the stems of wine glasses. They are particularly well represented in the Hubbard Collection. To give some idea of how well, and the colour range involved, a selection of the stems is shown here, plate 63.

As for other decoration, it was usually considered unnecessary to embellish the glasses further. With the exception of some incredibly rare pieces, such as the occasional Beilby, the bowls are mostly left undecorated or carry very light stylised engraving, so as not to detract from the vivid to soft pastel colouring displayed in the stems. Exceptions of course occur, as with the amusing hunting scene shown in this group, plate 67, page 54, and the floral and fruiting vine engraving of its companions. In plate 65 (opposite), the green in the stem of the small ovoid-bowled wine glass is rarely seen

without another colour. In size, wine glasses predominate, usually about 6ins high.

Cordials and goblets, plate 64 (opposite), are rarely found. A.C.'s great friend Harald Leuba has a fine selection. Colour was sometimes further enhanced by the addition of a column or cable of air, plates 68, 69 and 73, pages 55 and 56. With their subdued but striking decorative effect, these glasses are probably the high point in the art of creating stems with internal twists, one of the great challenges to the glassmakers' skills. The pair having turquoise on air twist stems, plate 73, page 56, also have beautifully engraved natural flowers. Knopping is rare, and not always effective, as it has sometimes distorted the internal enamel decoration to a disagreeable extent. Carefully selected, it can work very well, as in the case of these two bell bowled glasses, where it adds considerable interest, plate 70, page 56.

**Plate 63** *All of the glasses on pages 52-60 range in height from 5¹/₂ins - 7ins.*

The number of colours used, singly or in combination, is very large – blue, red, green, purple, orange and their shades. Rubber red, as in the left-hand glass, plate 67, page 54, is particularly attractive; a strong central column in white makes a striking background for the dark blue, plate 72, page 56.

The most sought after colour is yellow, which can vary in intensity from pale canary to a deep tone that is almost orange. It may appear in conjunction with other colours, plate 75, page 58. Here are two glasses, perhaps made by the same hand, one yellow and blue, the other amethyst with a yellow core. Plate 71, page 56, shows another yellow twist and in plate 74, page 57, a close-up of its stem appears with the mixed twist of plate 68, page 55. Also in the close-up, the stem of the Beilby privateer glass, plate 130, page 93, shows a startling combination.

Bowl shapes are mostly standard: bell, ogee, round funnel and trumpet predominating. The firing glasses of plate 79, page 59 are also rarities, though almost all cotton twist designs are matched in colour twists. I have not, however, encountered a terraced foot on a colour twist firing glass. This would make an interesting quarry for the collector/hunter, since I feel sure such glasses exist.

The drawn trumpet, plate 76, page 59, is probably unique, since it is a two-piece glass (close-up), plate 76, the bowl having apparently been formed from the clear glass at the top of the cone containing the coloured enamels from which the twist was to be formed. The skill and imagination required to execute this manoeuvre in molten glass – probably from a fortuitous first gather – is stunning. Plates 66 and 77, pages 54 and 59 show other interesting and unusual combinations of colour.

**Plate 64**

**Plate 65**

**Plate 66**, *page 53.*

**Plate 67**, *page 52.*

**Plate 68**, *page 52.*

**Plate 69**, *page 52.*

**Plate 71**, *page 53.*

**Plate 70**, *page 52.*

**Plate 72**, *page 53.*

**Plate 73**, *page 52.*

**Plate 74**, *page 53.*

**Plate 75**, *page 53.*

**Plate 76**, *page 53.*

**Plate 77**, *page 53.*

**Plate 78**, *page 53.  Close-up of plate 76, right.*

**Plate 79**, *page 53.  Three colour twist firing glasses, heights 4¹/₂ins, 4¹/₄ins and 4¹/₂ins.*

59

**Plate 80**  *Height 7¹/₄ins.*

# THE SWEETEST OF SWEETMEATS

Plate 80 is one of the princes in A.C.'s realm of glass, an example of the glassmaker's art so outstanding that only one possible outside rival is noted – and that out of private reach, in the Victoria and Albert Museum in London. It is used by Joseph Bles as the colour frontispiece for his famous book. A.C.'s lovely glass differs from this only in having an attractive leafy meander (perhaps mimosa) engraved on its bowl instead of the formal cross-hatching on the Victoria and Albert example. Amongst sweetmeats few others are noted with twist stems of any sort, much less in colour. One having (incredibly) a blue bowl and foot in addition to a colour twist stem is recorded, but this, sadly, was accidentally destroyed. Clearly, therefore, this is a piece to cherish above many others, not only for A.C.'s personal pleasure and that of those lucky enough to be allowed to see it, but for the benefit of future generations.

## FACETS – THE CUTTER COMES INTO HIS OWN

The earliest cutting on English wine glasses appeared on heavy balusters which seem to have been made for the purpose, perhaps in imitation of Bohemian and other German glass. The experiment was not particularly successful and these glasses occur infrequently. They are not really very attractive and do not appeal to collectors. More acceptable facet-cut designs, initially on stems alone, plates 82, page 62 and plate 124, page 91, appeared towards the middle of the eighteenth century, and as it progressed became more lavish, although the hollow geometric shapes used could never aspire technically to the elaboration of raised diamonds and other motifs that complicated the cutting of the next century. Such nineteenth century *tours-de-force* were sometimes to acquire a certain prickliness and over elaboration in design and texture that could occasion actual physical damage to the over-anxious hand of the drinker seizing a heavy decanter. No, the more subdued scales and honeycombs of eighteenth century cutting marvellously embellished while never threatening the user's grasp nor hurting his eye.

Cutting on stems quickly spread to the bases and the inner sections of feet, eventually, in rare examples of both wine and ale glasses, covering the glass completely, foot and all. The edge of the foot was sometimes elaborately scalloped as well, plate 83, page 62. But the extra effort of cutting was costly and tricky (it was all too easy to go through the wall of even a specially made bowl, which was not of uniform thickness), so the bowl and foot were most often left alone. The former might perhaps carry some basic engraving, frequently in the style now called 'OXO' from its polished dots and matt engraved 'Xs', or bear something slightly more elaborate such as vine leaves, polished hop and barley designs, flower sprigs, etc.

Special events were commemorated (as was usual) on whatever style of glass was fashionable at the time, such as this one commemorating the Treaty of Paris with beautiful polished engraving, plate 81, page 62, and the armorial engraved glass, plate 82, page 62, which may well be of Jacobite significance since (as happens with a few other facet glasses) on looking down into the bowl from directly above one can clearly see in the cutting the outline of a Stuart rose, plate 110, page 83. The armorial on this glass, however, has not been identified, but could be that of some family still clinging to Jacobite hopes. Facet wines are found with sophisticated engravings, plate 84, page 62, reflecting the highly fashionable style of the period, and other decorative scenes, sometimes specially commissioned.

The Dutch master engravers still sometimes used English facet-stemmed glasses for their exquisite work. One of the greatest and best known of these was David Wolff, but his skill with the diamond point was equalled and in some respects exceeded by the man (if it was a man) known only by the soubriquet 'Alius'. He signed nothing, but his work is so superior and idiosyncratic as to be unmistakable. It is beautifully exemplified by the close-up of this superb glass in the Collection, plate 86, page 63, and the glass itself, plate 85 on the same page.

**Fig. 26** *If you wanted something to put into your beautiful sweetmeat glasses, you would send to a confectioner like Alderman Hoare, who in the 1740s was supplying an incredible range of sweets and 'Desarts', shown here displayed on pyramids of tazzae. Guildhall Library, Corporation of London.*

**Plate 81**, *page 61. Height 6¹⁄₈ins.*

**Plate 82**, *page 61. Height both 6ins.*

**Plate 83**, *page 61. Heights 6¹⁄₄ins and 5ins.*

**Plate 84**, *page 61. Height 6ins.*

**Plate 85**, *page 61.*
*Height 7¹/₄ins.*

**Plate 86**, *page 61.*

63

**Fig. 27 and Fig. 28** *Maydwell and Windle's and William Parker's lavish rococo trade cards give some idea of the fashionable heights to which glass aspired (and had already achieved) by the second half of the eighteenth century. Much of their energies were devoted to cutting chandeliers, candelabra and candlesticks, larger pieces of table glass and services, but any 'curious cut, engravd' glass could be ordered, and 'plain glafses of all sorts' were available. The words 'for exportation' are often included, so it would be perfectly possible for some of A.C.'s bottles and glasses to have reached America shortly after they were made. Parker's card is surmounted by a magnificent centrepiece for sweetmeats (called a sweetmeat tree) and illustrates tantalising glimpses of knopped, lidded and engraved glasses. © Copyright The British Museum.*

AT
*Maydwell and Windles*
CUT-GLASS Warehouse, The KING's-ARMS
Against Norfolk-Street in the STRAND
LONDON,
Are Made and Sold all Sorts of Curious Glass-Work,
Fine Scollop'd Lustrees & Fine Scollop'd Fountains
Branch Candlesticks & Muggs & Covers
Services for Deserts & Travelling Cases
Bowls & Covers & Essence Bottles
Dishes & Plates & Cruet Frames
Engraving on Glasses of ev'ry kind in the
Newest Taste at y' most Reasonable Rates.
LIKEWISE SELL
Plain Glasses of all Sorts.

HONI SOIT QUI MAL Y PENSE
DIEU ET MON DROIT

R.ᵈ Clee Fecit.

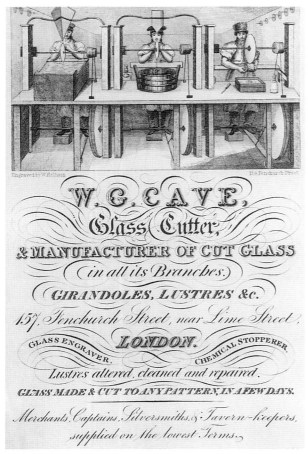

**Fig. 29** *Mr. Cave offered a diverse range of services to an equally diverse list of trade customers. The treadle drive used for the cutting and engraving wheels was common until well into the nineteenth century. Guildhall Library, Corporation of London.*

**Fig. 30** *John Jacob's beautiful trade card, dated 1775 includes 'newest pattern drinking glasses', presumably facet cut like those illustrated here in A.C.'s Collection. © Copyright The British Museum.*

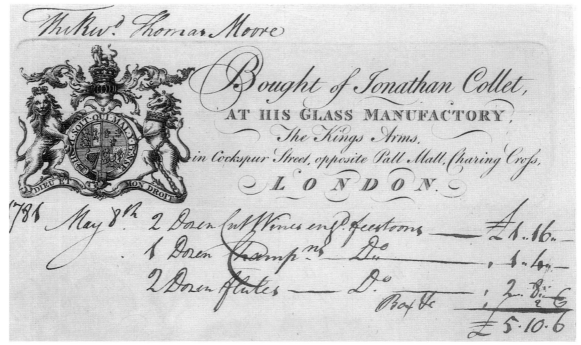

**Fig. 31** *What type of glasses, one wonders, were for champagne? Clearly not flutes. Eighteenth century champagne was drunk flat, since it could be decanted, as labelled decanters of the date show us. And why were flutes so much more expensive than the wine glasses, which were cut and engraved with festoons? The clergy of the time might drink as heartily as the gentry, but the Revd. Moore, at least, settled his bills. Francis Buckley suggests that 'flutes' were flute-cut wine glasses, which perhaps accounts for the price differential. © Copyright The British Museum.*

# GLASS IN THE HANDS OF THE PAINTER DECORATORS AND DECORATING – THE BEILBYS AND OTHERS

The main attraction of Beilby glasses lies in their originality. True, the Beilbys most certainly took commissions from vainglorious patrons and others: what eighteenth century artist did not? Such orders ranged from large, full-colour armorials and crests on decanters, bowls and goblets, to the emblems of masonic and other societies and clubs. But the real beauty of their work is found in the marvellous little vignettes they painted, usually on the bowls of small glasses, sometimes even tiny cordials, depicting all manner of things, from classical ruins to everyday life, birds and flowers, sports and pastimes, rural scenes... conceits as unique in inspiration as they are charming in execution. Of course, they also picked up on the standard designs of the day – fruiting vine, hops and barley, floral sprigs and such features were also used by contemporary wheel engravers. When required, they would apply and embellish in white enamel (perhaps heightened with a little pale blue) the names of wines and other beverages on decanters of shouldered and mallet shapes – frequently magnums or larger.

As with ceramics, the high temperatures at which the enamels were fired, close to the melting point of glass, were difficult to control and there may have been considerable kiln loss. We do not know how substantial this was, but one sometimes encounters Beilby glasses where the bowl has slightly collapsed or gone awry, or where stem or foot is marginally distorted. Sometimes one sees a pontil-mark inside the bowl, placed there to hold the glass while any slight distortion is corrected. The gilding that one finds on the rims of Beilby glasses has in most instances virtually disappeared. It does not seem to have been as effectively fired on as are the enamels and has consequently worn away with use. Light crazing of the enamel also sometimes occurs, and an occasional example may show slight brown discolouration.

In the following article, my friend and colleague Simon Cottle skillfully outlines and discusses the historical background, the known biographical details, certain specific glass designs, and some of the working practices of the Beilby family.

# WILLIAM BEILBY AND THE ART OF GLASS PAINTING

## *by Simon Cottle*

Perhaps of all eighteenth century English drinking glasses, those which attract the most attention – and certainly some of the highest prices at auction – are the masterpieces of enamelling produced by the Beilby workshop at Newcastle-upon-Tyne. Three hundred or more examples survive from what was a short-lived renaissance of the art of glass enamelling in England. This was an art form which, apart from the contemporary decorators on opaque-white glass in the South Staffordshire industry, was unrivalled by other English enamellers of glass. For the history of glass enamelling one has to look to the Continent – particularly to Venice and the German provinces – where the technique was practised from the end of the fifteenth century, especially in association with gilding. Apart from a mere handful of examples, enamelling on vessel glass in England was little known until the emergence of the Beilbys. One of the earliest examples is the water carafe inscribed *Thos. Worrall 1757*, which is now at Broadfield House Glass Museum, Kingswinford.

At the end of the 1750s, a Durham silversmith, William Beilby, Sr. (1706-65) fell on hard times and moved northwards to the prosperous port of Newcastle-upon-Tyne. His wife, Mary (1712-78) joined him, together with four of his children. They settled just south of the River Tyne in Gateshead where, until his death in 1765, William continued his trade as a silversmith and jeweller. That might have been the end of the story. However, the Northumbrian woodcut artist, Thomas Bewick, famous for his pastoral, animal and ornithological vignettes and studies of local life, published in his memoir (1822) a report of how William's children assisted greatly in the recovery of the family's fortunes. The text of that memoir referring to the Beilbys is worth reading in full, as it is one of the few surviving pieces of documentary evidence about the family:

*'The father of this family followed the business of a Goldsmith and Jeweller in Durham – where he had been greatly respected, he had taken care to give all his family a good education – his eldest Son Richard had served his apprenticeship to a die sinker or seal Engraver in Birmingham – his second son William had also learned enamelling and painting in the same place – the former of these had taught my master R.(alph) seal cutting and the latter taught their brother Thomas and sister Mary, enamelling and painting – and in this way this most industrious and respectable family, lived together and maintained themselves – but prior to this state of things, while the family were more dependant upon the industry of their father he failed in business, left Durham and begun business in Gateshead where he, as well as his eldest son Richard died.*

*About this period I was informed, that the family had to struggle with great difficulties and that by way of helping to get through them, their mother taught a school in Gateshead – but this state of things could not last long, for the industrial ingenuity and the united energies of the family, must soon have enabled them to soar above every obstacle – My master had wrought as a jeweller, with his father before he went to his brother Richard to learn Seal cutting which was only for a very short time before his death – He also assisted his Brothers and Sister, in the constant employment of painting upon glass'.*

Thus we learnt that William, Jr. (1740-1819), Ralph (1743-1817), Thomas (1747-1826) and Mary Beilby (1749-?) worked in the heart of Newcastle at Amen Corner, in the shadow of the cathedral church of St. Nicholas'. At this workshop the children applied their different skills to a range of material from engraved printing plates and engraved silver to the decorating of glass with enamels. It is probable that the enamelling was undertaken at a local glasshouse of which there were several along the banks of the River Tyne nearby. However, as some doubt has been cast on whether glass of such high quality was made in Newcastle at the time, the glass may have been imported from London or even Holland. The manner in which the enamel and gilt decoration was fired onto the surface of the glass would suggest that a hot furnace and an annealing or muffle kiln were required and it is unlikely that this would be available to them at their Amen Corner workshop.

It is believed that William had originally been apprenticed to John Haseldine, decorator of enamel boxes in Birmingham between 1755-60. Either Haseldine or William's training may have provided the inspiration for his later trade. Although John Haseldine is mentioned in the Birmingham Directory of 1767 as a Drawing Master and is not shown as an enameller, he may, nonetheless, have started life as a box enameller at Bilston nearby.

The Beilbys decorated a small amount of polychrome enamelled glass in the first few years of the workshop's existence, probably to commission. This consisted largely of single or pairs of goblets and decanters finely painted with armorial decoration. There are also a couple of large punchbowls, one painted with a ship – The Margaret and Winneford – dating from the launch of the vessel in April, 1767, light baluster wine glasses, and firing glasses. This last group generally bears Masonic devices. Whilst some of the armorials may be fictitious, the majority have been positively identified and their owners stretch from Buckinghamshire, Kent and Devon in the south of England to Yorkshire, Cumberland, Scotland and Wales in the north and west.

In form, the goblets are typically bucket-shaped and are set on opaque twist stems with generous conical feet. It may have been a happy coincidence that the fashion for this type of glass coincided with the Beilbys' enamelling period or perhaps it was their inspiration. The elegant polychrome or coloured variety of Beilby glass incorporating armorials and gilt decoration appears to have been produced between circa 1762 and circa 1770. Alongside this production, or perhaps somewhat later, the workshop was responsible for a larger series of glasses, making up the bulk of the now existing glass, painted solely in opaque white enamel. Gilt edging or the traces of gilding can be found on the rims of many of the lesser glasses. Wine glasses, goblets, tumblers, decanters, bowls and flasks provided the canvases for either fruiting vine – the most common image – pastoral scenes, landscapes, sporting images, classical ruins or inscriptions, or a combination of these themes. The painting is exquisite and well detailed, the artists capturing a study of pastoral life in a most charming manner. Of the polychrome variety, the earliest dated example is the magnificent *Standard of Hesleyside*, 1763, bearing the arms of Major Edward Charlton, from an old Northumberland family. Standing almost 12ins tall, the *Standard* was a type of competition glass, the challenge being to drink the contents – a full-size bottle of wine –

at one attempt without spilling a drop. A hollow knop in the stem acted like the bulb at the end of a 'yard of ale'. The so-called 'Standard' was obviously difficult to achieve. A number of splendid goblets and decanters painted with the arms of George III and the triple feather badge of the Prince of Wales may be of earlier manufacture. They probably commemorate the birth of George, Prince of Wales (later King George IV), in August 1762. One unusual example is painted with a ship on one side – either for the 'Prince George' or 'King George' – the arms of George III on the other and is inscribed *Success to the African trade of WHITEHAVEN*. Coincidentally, the third mate on the Prince George was John Paul Jones, the American revolutionary, who later returned with the rebel navy to lay siege to Whitehaven itself! For some years this glass held the auction record for a Beilby glass, prior to the sale of the Buckmaster Goblet by Sotheby's in December 1997. It probably commemorates the slaving ship named after the Prince of Wales, which was launched at the time of his birth. It is also understood that the ship was owned by John Spedding, the owner of three slave ships and an agent for the Earl of Lonsdale, a cousin of King George III, hence the Royal arms. Unlike most Beilby glass, this example is signed *Beilby junr invt. and Pinxit*. There are several signed pieces extant and in addition some are inscribed with the name of the town of Newcastle. Those signed pieces include goblets, decanters and a large punchbowl. Since William Beilby, Jr. dropped the suffix after his father died in March 1765, glass bearing that fuller signature can be dated a little more precisely.

Whilst the variety and origin of many of the more important armorials and crests not only indicates the growing and wide popularity of the Beilby's work, they may also provide the clues as to why the glasses were commissioned in the first place. Looking closely at the individuals to whom the glasses belonged, the common thread appears to be political. The armorials included those of Members of Parliament, aristocrats, leading clerics, mayors and town councillors. The word-of-mouth recommendation – perhaps from Edward Blackett or another north-eastern MP – may have helped secure a number of commissions from parliamentarians in the south of England.

It has been suggested that William may have been enamelling glass in Birmingham prior to the opening of the workshop in Newcastle. The existence of a tankard dated 1760, which may be William's work, and a series of inscribed baluster-shaped opaque white scent flasks might also provide evidence to support this theory. Much of the credit for their enamelled glass should perhaps go to William Beilby, Jr. but Bewick records that he was ably assisted by his brothers and sister and the workshop appears to have been a collaborative affair, particularly in the second half of the 1760s.

Taking this fact into account, I believe that William's younger brother, Thomas, played a far more important part in the decorating of the glass than is generally acknowledged. Like William, he was a drawing master and an artist of some repute in Newcastle until he left the town in 1769. Ralph was an heraldic specialist and must have at least advised on, or drawn the designs for, some of the armorials. Before her paralytic stroke, which occurred about 1774 and is mentioned by Bewick, Mary must also have played an important role in the workshop. Her background is, however, sketchy. Bewick described how she had been taught the art of enamelling, so we must assume that some of the glass was decorated by her. Perhaps some of the more delicate floral banded glasses and the fruiting vines may be from her hand but I do not believe that she was involved to any great extent in the more complex and detailed polychrome production from the earlier period. She would have been only eleven years of age when the workshop was established in 1760 and I feel it unlikely that she was involved in the decorating of glass until she was older.

Thomas Beilby's departure from Newcastle at the end of the 1760s perhaps provides the dividing line between the period of polychrome and that of opaque white enamelling. It is likely that some monochrome examples were produced before 1769, but their more intensive production probably occurred after that date and at least until 1774. The survival of a tumbler in the Corning Museum of Glass inscribed *M BELL 1778* indicates that the workshop's enamelling production continued until the date of their departure for London, albeit sporadically.

Bewick records elsewhere in his memoir that William and Thomas were drawing masters. Indeed, William established a drawing school in Newcastle in 1767 and following his departure from the town in 1778 he founded another such school (the Battersea Academy) in London. Both he and Thomas toured Northumberland painting together and some of their paintings are in major collections in America and the United Kingdom. There are a number of parallels between William's enamelling work and his water-colour drawings. Some of the pastoral vignettes on Beilby glass, such as those depicting figures of shepherds, gnarled oak trees, animals, cottages, etc. are portrayed in both media. Though there are no existing parallels between Thomas' perhaps more distinctive hand in water-colour and any white enamelled glass, water-colour cartouches signed by Thomas show that he contributed to the design for the outlines of some of the armorial glasses. A water-colour cartouche similar to that for the Couper Goblet in the Cinzano collection, for example, may be seen in the Laing Art Gallery, Newcastle-upon-Tyne.

It has also been suggested that Thomas Bewick provided much of the inspiration for the decoration in white enamel. Whilst he may well have brought some ideas to the workshop, his apprenticeship to Ralph Beilby in 1767, at the tender age of 14, probably pre-dates much of his acclaimed work and it seems much more likely that he was inspired by his mentors instead. The pastoral vignettes in white enamel relate closely to William Beilby's water-colour drawings and, curiously, to a small and rare group of bucket-bowled goblets painted in polychrome with landscapes. Several of these glasses have been recorded and are mostly in the hands of American museums. An unrecorded pair with either a shepherd or shepherdess remains in private hands in the United Kingdom. These glasses may provide the natural link between the polychrome armorial and the monochrome enamel glass. The other images on the wine glasses are typical of motifs found on porcelain at this time and it would be a mistake to judge Beilby glass in isolation from the other decorative arts and the fashions of the period. The use of the fruiting vine motif is a classic image engraved on drinking glasses and decanters, whilst the simulated wine labels – pendant on the shoulders of decanters – are an indication of the popularity for the silver equivalent at the time. The use of a butterfly, suggested by some as a signature for William Beilby, is an accepted device both in glass and porcelain for hiding a piece of grit in the glass or a flaw in the porcelain.

Curiously, a group of glass has survived which have possible continental associations. A light baluster wine glass in the Victoria and Albert Museum for example has allusions in the polychrome crest to French wine growing. Similarly, two light baluster glasses with the arms of the House of Orange appear to be copies of a popular commemorative theme commonly found engraved on Dutch glass. Apart from the yet to be accepted suggestion that many of their glass blanks were imported from the continent, the answer to this might lie amidst evidence that William Beilby apparently embarked on a tour of Holland and of the Rhine before he left Newcastle in 1778. Some water-colours and pencil drawings with views of canals and other continental scenes have survived. Some may have been executed while William was living in London. Nonetheless, a visit to northern Europe would also have provided William with the opportunity to obtain commissions for glass enamelling.

With the Beilbys going in different directions, by 1778 the workshop had fragmented and the enamelling side of the business was curtailed. William's mother Mary died in that year and we know that he continued to look after his ailing young sister. Thomas was now living close to Sheffield before moving to Birmingham, and Ralph had embarked on an independent career as an engraver. The year 1778 is significant, too, in that it is said that opaque twist glass which had been exempt from the Glass Excise Tax – first levied on the weight of the glass in 1745 – was extended to cover such glasses, thus making them more expensive. I am not certain if this is true. If it is the case, it will not have helped the producers of enamelled glass.

William Beilby moved to London where he is recorded in Battersea in 1779. Here he met Ellen Turton whom he later married, and became a respected member of the local parish council. With Mary, William and Ellen later moved to Scotland to manage her uncle's estates and then finally to Hull in 1814, where William died shortly after – on 9th October, 1819. Bewick records that 'Long after this she [Mary] went with her eldest brother into Fifeshire, where she died'. It is unlikely that William produced any further enamelled glass after he left Newcastle.

Thus with William's death, the seal was set on a short period of English glass which in the treatment of the enamel decoration has only been matched by continental artisans working within a much longer tradition. To gain an insight into the stylistic variation of each of the members of the workshop, in the absence of documentary evidence, Beilby glass needs to be examined closely. Their success was to have mastered the firing of the enamels so that the decoration remains for the most part in the same condition as the day the glass left the workshop.

*Simon Cottle*
*Director European Ceramics and Glass*
*Sotheby's, London*

# THE KING OF A.C.'S CASTLE
## THE DUTCH ROYAL ARMORIAL GOBLET

This glass, plate 87, was first offered for sale at Sotheby's on 15th December, 1975, catalogued as follows:
"A HIGHLY IMPORTANT ROYAL GOBLET ENAMELLED WITH THE ARMS OF THE HOUSE OF ORANGE by William Beilby, signed, the deep round-funnel bowl with internal pontil, supported on a typical Newcastle stem, the bowl superbly enamelled on one side with the arms of Nassau Princes of Orange encircled by the ribbon below the arms bearing the motto of the Princes of Orange JE MAIN TIEN DRAY, the reverse with a white butterfly in profile beneath the signature in red, Beilby Newcastle pinxt., 11ins, circa 1766.

From the collection of the present owner's grandmother, Mme. Leon Possemiers.

It seems likely that this magnificent goblet was enamelled in Newcastle for presentation to prince William V of Orange

**Plate 87** *The Beilby, Dutch Royal Armorial Goblet, height 11³/₄ins.*

**Plate 88** *The Beilby inscription and the white butterfly in close-up of the reverse of plate 87, page 71.*

on attaining his majority at the age of eighteen in 1766, and before his marriage to Wilhelmina of Prussia in 1767, after this date it would have been normal to have had the arms of his wife as well.

The date proposed also fits in with what is understood to have been the practise of William Beilby in omitting 'Jr' from his signature after the death of his father in 1765.

William V of Orange was born in March 1748, son of William IV and Anne, daughter of George II. His mother acted as regent until her death on 12th January 1759 when the Provincial States took over these duties, at the same time Duke Louise Ernest of Brunswick-Wolfenbuttel was appointed guardian. William was declared of age in 1766 and remained Stadtholder until 1795. He has been described as Anglophile and incompetent. He died in Brunswick in 1806.

Two other goblets of Dutch interest enamelled by William Beilby are recorded. The first was a goblet with the arms of the Dutch family Tilley of Harleem, sold in these rooms 1st July 1949, lot 16. The second goblet which like the present one is remarkable for the presence of the pontil mark on the inside of the bowl is enamelled with the arms of Van Dongen of Huisden, Zeeland. For an English Royal Goblet by Beilby also sold at Sotheby's, see catalogue 14th July 1975, lot 224. See also Wilfred Buckley 'Anglo-Dutch Glasses of the XVIII Century, Old Furniture', July 1928, fig X, W.A. Thorpe, 'The Beilby Glasses' Connoisseur May 1928, fig. XIII (for a goblet of almost identical form to the present) and Hugh Tait, 'The Pilkington Glass Museum' Connoisseur December 1964, for the Van Dongen glass mentioned above".

The glass was again offered at Sotheby's on 1st November 1982. It spent some time in America before returning to London, to be purchased by A.C.

## THE BEST LOVED OF THE FAMILY

It would perhaps be an appropriate introduction to the rest of A.C.'s magnificent Collection of Beilbys if we looked first at a glass we have previously mentioned – one of the few glass treasures which A.C. intends to retain in his family. Because of his sentimental attachment to duck shooting and because of his initial (mistaken), belief that the sportsman depicted here (like A.C. himself) was shooting off his left shoulder, this glass, plate 89, is especially dear to A.C.'s heart.

The charming vignette it presents is a good example of the Beilbys' fondness for showing everyday subjects – shepherds and sheep, farming and gardening, little landscapes, boating, sports, and so on – as well as a whole series of their beloved classical ruins, all of which are virtually unique decorative subjects on eighteenth century glass.

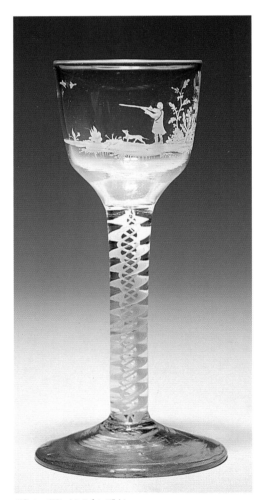

**Plate 89** *Height 5⁷/₈ins.*

This introduction having given a glimpse of one of the joys of collecting – the direct personal appeal to the heart – we are now led to turn our attention to A.C'.s other Beilbys in all their splendour, and foremost among these must come the examples in glowing colour.

As well as the great William of Orange Newcastle armorial that we have just looked at, we find in the Collection another glass bearing heraldic decoration, this time a simpler device of red stars and a blue chevron on a white ground. The glass, plate 91, is a fine bucket bowled goblet with gilt rim and ruined arches and an 'Adam' pyramid in white on the side opposite the armorial. The arms are those of Pollard.

Two further highly important colour decorated Beilby glasses in the Collection – a Jacobite and a privateer – are illustrated under the appropriate headings, see pages 75 and 93. First we look at some of the very select pieces decorated in simple monochrome white or white and gilt, but miracles of miniature painting just the same, and deserving of the closest attention.

It was unusual for the Beilbys to decorate anything other than drinking glasses and the occasional decanter, so this bowl, plate 90, is indeed a striking exception. It is doubly interesting in also being dated – obviously a commission – and it may one day be traced. The scrolls and diaper tracery of the painting mirror engraved design of the day.

Yet another example of the wide range of the Beilbys' work is this fine magnum mallet decanter, in superb condition, painted with hops and barley ears, and carrying the gilt label 'BEER' – in itself a name unusual on any decanter or decanter label, 'ALE' being for some reason more often found, though still rarely. This magnificent piece is 14½ins high, plate 92, page 74.

Flanking the decanter are a pair of splendid goblets, with full vine decoration and – most surprisingly – also having matching lids, fully decorated, plate 92a, page 75. No other such pair are known to exist. Unlike their continental cousins, English drinking glasses were not usually fitted with lids, and in any case most of those that were have had their lids lost or broken. (The first part of this statement is not entirely borne out by the advertisements in this book). These splendid goblets, recently discovered, are therefore a collector's dream come true. Being lidded, they may well have been made for export. Also, they came from an old Dutch family. Their overall height is 9¾ins.

One cannot leave the subject of Beilby decoration without reference to their classical and gothic ruins, a beautiful example being shown here on the right of plate 98, page 77, together with two of the pagoda-like

**Plate 90**
*Diam. 5ins.*

**Plate 91**  *Height 7¾ins.*

73

**Plate 92**, *page 73.  Height decanter 14¹/₂ins, goblets 9³/₄ins.*

Plate 92a , *page 73.*

Plate 93, *page 77.   Height 7⅝ins.*

**Plate 94**, *page 77.   Heights 7¼ins and  7⅛ins.*

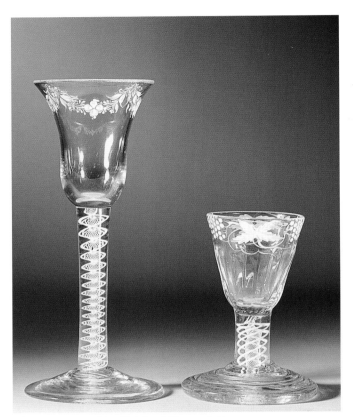

**Plate 95**, *page 77.   Height 6⅜ins and 4ins.*

**Plate 96**, *page 77.   Height 4ins.*

**Plate 97**, *page 77.*

**Plate 98** *Heights 5³/₄ins.*

architectural structures, inhabited by the little dreamlike chinoiserie figures which the fertile Beilby imagination conjured up.

The decorative devices and types of glass they regularly used are numerous. A few more of A.C.'s specimens from the range are shown here, two ales, over 7ins high, one decorated with a diaper pattern, the other floral, heightened with turquoise, plate 94. Plate 95 shows two very different glasses, respectively decorated with floral swags and fruiting vines. Note the rare terraced feet on the firing glasses.

Jacobite subjects were not commonly required by Beilby patrons – or possibly the Beilbys were reluctant to accept such commissions. For whatever reason, this ale, plate 93, page 75 – decorated in vivid colors – is a really exceptional glass in every respect. The crowned thistle and its inscription NEMO ME IMPUNE LACESSIT seem to put its Jacobite significance beyond doubt. Its fellow can be found in the Philadelphia Museum. No others are recorded. An exceptionally rare polychrome Beilby in

A.C.'s Collection, the 'Providence' glass, will be found illustrated plates 130 and 131, page 93.

The amusing injunction to 'TEMPERANCE', not much followed in the eighteenth century, decorates the (probably) unique little air twist deceptively bowled firing glass of plate 96. The unmistakable, elegantly painted scrolling of the Beilby hand is seen in close-up on plate 97, where the bowl is filled with wine.

## THE BRUSH IN DIFFERENT HANDS

There were other enamellers working in England at about the same time as the Beilbys, but none who came near them in technique, artistic merit or output.

The prettily named and dated mug in the centre of the plate 99, page 78 is a nice example of 'SUCCESS TO...' more ordinary people than pirates or politicians – in this case perhaps the landlord of an inn and his wife. As the

**Plate 99**, *page 77.    Heights 3¹/₂ins, 5¹/₄ins and 3³/₄ins.*

**Plate 100**, *page 79.    Heights 5³/₄ins, 5⁷/₈ins and 5³/₄ins.*

bottle section of this book will show, landlords' wives, unlike those of many other social stations, enjoyed equal importance to the man himself. Although the date makes an attribution tempting, the mug is probably not Beilby decorated.

The other two pieces in plate 99, are not Beilby work. The masonic terraced foot firing glass is decorated by a recognisable hand, but not one to which anyone has yet been able to put a name. The other little rarity may tentatively be attributed to Giles, as I will discuss in a moment.

Mention may also be made of a very rare type of enamelling which may or may not be the work of the Beilbys. This is wash enamelling – a thinly applied coat of white enamel paint, fired on, which does not at first glance appear to be enamel at all. The technique with which this was done is very good, but the subject is familiar, since (as far as I know) it is solely fruiting vine. I can best describe its appearance by telling of my first encounter with it – some glasses (three, I think), were on a market stall in Bermondsey, the famous outdoor antiques market in London. It was early, the light was not good, and I bought this quite handsome trio of 'cotton twists' assuming (as I expect did the stall-holder), that they were nicely engraved eighteenth century glasses, sold at a price one would expect to pay. Viewed later in better light, I realised they were enamelled, but one had to look quite closely to recognise the fact. Naturally I was pleased to find such rarities, but I could not help wondering why anyone should use this technique, since the enamel was clearly fired on (with attendant risk), and the result was not superior in appearance to less-risky engraving. But I suppose that this speculation in itself explains the rarity of the work.

A.C. has a nice example, a recent acquisition plate 100 (opposite, centre), enamelled with fruiting vine, on a double series air twist stem. The other two are beautifully Beilby painted with a rural neo-classical scene and buildings in a rustic landscape. Wash enamel does appear on some Beilby decanters, together with the more usual thick glossy painting.

Because of its similarity in style and appearance to the decoration of porcelain known to emanate from there, gilding on clear glass is assumed to come from the London workshop of James Giles. Though examples in the Giles manner come on the market from time to time, it is a treat to see a gilded ale glass in such immaculate condition as this one from the Collection, plate 101. White and other coloured glass was also gilded by Giles, often with very characteristic Greek paterae and bucrania (stylised ox skulls), connected by floral-inspired swags – a system of decor sometimes emulated by engravers on facet glasses and perhaps coming from the same source.

**Plate 101** *Heights 5¹/₄ins and 7¹/₂ins.*

# THE JACOBITES:
# THEIR FAMILY AND FRIENDS...

Because of their Roman Catholicism, the Stuart dynasty was debarred by Act of Parliament from assuming the throne of England after Queen Anne's death in 1714. Although it was their right by birth, the so-called Act of Settlement, signed by Anne (a staunch Protestant) in 1701, prevented their succession and guaranteed the throne to George I, the Elector of Hanover, whose claim to it was through a Protestant line.

For long after, indeed well into the nineteenth century, the Stuarts had strong support for their claims. Initially this took the form of armed struggle (or rebellion as the then rulers called it) resulting in the uprisings of 1715 (led by James Edward Stuart, the Old Pretender) and 1745 (the Young Pretender, better known as 'Bonnie Prince Charlie'). Many Jacobite clubs (so called after King James II) were formed, initially politically and militarily dangerous in intent, but degenerating towards the end of the century into mere social and drinking clubs, with little if any clout. Earlier, belonging to these clubs was risky, but since many prominent figures, including dukes, were known to have Jacobite sympathies, the authorities largely (and sensibly) ignored their activities. The Cycle Club, the Society of Sea Sergeants and others carried on carousing, toasting the Stuarts, making blood-curdling threats (behind closed doors, of course), and in general enjoying themselves thoroughly.

These clubs and Stuart-supporting families commissioned quantities of engraved glassware. Since such engraving could not show overt support for the cause many symbols were brought into use. The main one was the Stuart rose

**Fig. 32** *'The Young Pretender'.*

and bud, but many others were employed. Examples are the Boscobel Oak (in which James II hid after losing the Battle of Worcester), a riven oak stump, a sunburst and a moth (which for some imponderable reason signifies a return to Scotland, the land of Stuart roots). There are many Latin tags of vague or ambiguous meaning, like FIAT (let it be), REDEAT (he returns), REVIRESCIT (may he come back), TURNO TEMPUS ERIT (the times change), AUDENTIOR IBO (really meaningless, probably a mis-spelling of Audentior Bibo – I drink boldly), and others. A.C.'s splendid Beilby ale has the Scottish loyal Jacobite motto 'Nemo me Impune Lacefsit', illustrated in plate 93, page 75. There are some rare examples where defiant Jacobites seem to have invited trouble. Earliest of these are the famous 'Amen' glasses, diamond-point engraved with the Jacobite national anthem. They date from after the 1715 uprising and a small number can be fully authenticated as having remained since then in the same families. Other unprovenanced examples may well be genuine, but should be viewed with some care. Further outspoken rarities carry a portrait of Bonnie Prince Charlie, see plate 107, page 82 (shown together with a two-piece air twist engraved with a very thorny rose) or (in one unique instance), that of Flora Macdonald, who famously helped Charlie's escape by rowing him 'over the seas to Skye', after his loss of the Battle of Culloden (1745).

For long after the Jacobite cause was totally lost and its leaders fled overseas, the romantic-minded, still under the spell of the Stuarts' undoubted charm, would sometimes openly drink toasts to 'The King over the water', passing their glasses over a symbolic bowl of water.

**Plate 102**, *page 83.   Heights 7ins and 7¹/₈ins.*

**Plate 103**,
*page 83.*
*Height 6¹/₄ins.*

**Plate 104**, *page 83.   Heights both 6³/₄ins.*

**Plate 105**, *opposite and page 84.    Heights both 6¹⁄₂ins.*

**Plate 106**, *page 84.    Heights 3ins and 7³⁄₄ins.*

**Plate 107**, *opposite.    Heights 6³⁄₈ins and 6¹⁄₈ins.*

**Plate 108**, *opposite and page 84.    Heights 6ins and 6¹⁄₂ins.*

**Plate 109** *Height 7⁷/₈ins.*

more specifically Jacobite than its companion, which carries flower and fly decoration, perhaps hinting at its bias.

Glasses of earlier date (some of which probably refer to the Old Pretender) were also used, the commonest being the plain stemmed drawn trumpet and its air twist follower of the same shape. Even light balusters like plates 102 and 103, page 81, were used to carry carefully veiled references. Giants like the goblet, plate 109, pretty forcefully conveyed the sympathies of the owner – the bold decoration could hardly be misunderstood. Even more specific were glasses with the sort of inscriptions I have already discussed, although these also could be misconstrued, plate 104, page 81. The unquenchable optimism of the Jacobite supporter gives a ring to certain phrases that seems to make them recognisable. Of course there is room for error, but somehow 'He Shines every where' instantly conjures up the image of the Bonnie Prince, plate 103, page 81. The Scottish thistle is one of the recognised ambivalent symbols of the Stuart cause, especially when combined with the rose, plate 108 (opposite). Here the crowned lion unmistakably suggests the engraver's (or his patron's) view of the correct place for a Stuart king to be – on the throne of England. The other glass also shows a crown and rose and thistle (again uniting Stuart with throne) springing from the same stem.

Knopped air twists were typical glasses used to convey Jacobite sentiments, plate 105 (opposite). The rose and bud glass again bears the most usual Jacobite injunction 'Fiat'. There are not many still available. The floral motifs on the other glass may or may not be Jacobite. To express your loyalty to the Stuart cause unmistakably, however, you needed a portrait glass like plate 107 (opposite), not, you will note, of his father, the 'Old Pretender', who was still alive, nor his elder brother, Prince Henry, who was to

Some outstanding Jacobite glasses have found their way into the Collection. Let's look at a few of the finest:

Jacobite activity between the failure of the 1715 rebellion and that of 1745 does not appear to have been much recorded on glass – possibly because James Stuart (the Old Pretender) lacked the romantic image of his son Charles (the Young Pretender). The flowering of the movement (at least as far as glass decoration is concerned) is post Culloden. The double knopped air twist, plate 105 (opposite), with its rose and bud and the inscription 'FIAT' is rarer than the more usual drawn trumpet shape. It is

**Plate 110**, *page 84.*

become a cardinal. No, Charles Edward Stuart was the charmer whose portrait on glass was engraved after contemporary prints like Fig. 32. He was to remain well loved until his death and after, as can be seen in later glasses like plates 106 and 108, page 82.

Even at the end of the eighteenth century, facet glasses were being used to stir up memories of him. Look from directly above into the bowls of some of them to see the hidden Stuart rose in the base of the bowl, outlined by the cutting, plate 110, page 83 – a truly cunning way of expressing one's loyalties!

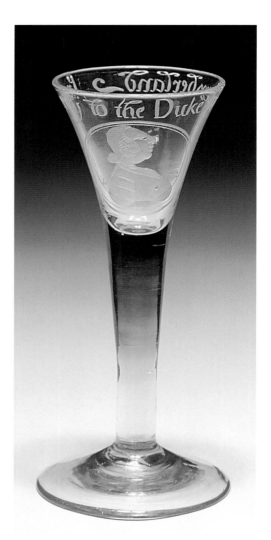

**Plate 112**  *Height 6³/₈ins.*

## ... AND THEIR ENEMIES

Culloden, and later, produced the most menacing Jacobite enemy of all – the Duke of Cumberland (known throughout Scotland as 'Butcher Cumberland'), son of George II. He was lauded on glass by English royalists, who had been badly frightened by Bonnie Prince Charlie and his army.

Having won the battle in 1745, Cumberland put down the rebellion with great savagery. Here is his portrait, plate 112, on a plain stemmed drawn trumpet glass and on a beautifully engraved heavy baluster goblet, plate 111. But the first Jacobite enemies were, of course, the late seventeenth and early eighteenth century queens of England – those ruling after James II that is – in spite of the fact that they themselves were Stuarts (Queen Mary, wife of William III, and Queen Anne, both daughters of James II). My colleague Alan Milford here provides some of the background.

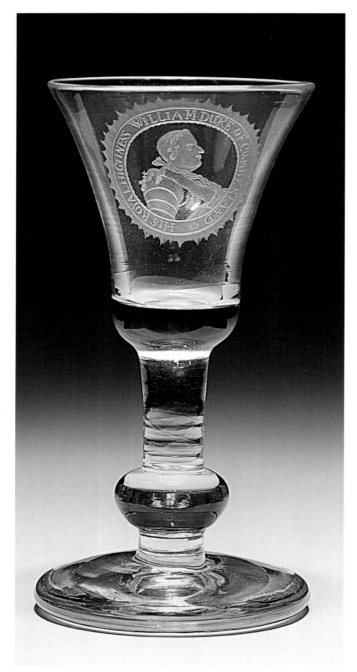

**Plate 111**  *Height 6¹/₂ins.*

# THE ORANGE CONNECTION
## by Alan Milford

*Having been heavily involved in helping A.C. form his Collection of drinking glasses and related articles, I thought I might also help Ward by writing a small chapter. I told A.C. that, for a large fee, I would be willing to do this. A.C. offered instead a meal at Charleston, the fine local restaurant in which he has an interest. I jumped at this 'fee', since A.C. keeps a few bottles of fine wine there, and he doesn't yet know what I'm going to order!*

In 1688, William of Orange, Stadthouder of the United Provinces of Holland, married Mary, eldest daughter of James II. By this time, James had brought unpopularity upon himself by converting to Roman Catholicism, a course of action that was to cost him his throne, lost when his son-in-law William was invited to invade and become, jointly with his wife Queen Mary, monarchs of England. They ruled firstly as William and Mary, then – after her death – as William III. Many artifacts have survived from this turbulent period and amongst A.C.'s glasses are some notable rarities associated with it, plates 113 and 116, pages 86 and 87.

One of the most important is this hollow quatrefoil-knopped goblet with gadrooned bowl. It is of full lead glass and is of well recognised form. The majority of such glasses are in museums, and many are heavily crizzled. This example is only very lightly affected, hence the rare feature of both Stuart and Orange-Nassau arms can be clearly seen, the former surrounded by roses and the latter by oranges, suggesting that it was engraved to celebrate the marriage of William and Mary, which would date it at 1688. These goblets were always called 'Hawley Bishopp', after the then proprietor of the Savoy glasshouse in London, successor to George Ravenscroft. The majority of British collectors would not admit that lead glass (which they claimed was Ravenscroft's discovery) was in use elsewhere. It is only recently that research has shown that it was also being produced in at least four other places in Northern Europe at the same time. Another piece dating from this period is this small tumbler in heavy, clear greyish lead glass, with a high kick base, that is probably English. It is deeply engraved with William's arms, as borne when he became King of England. There does not appear to be another like it, plate 115, page 87.

A great rarity, recently discovered in the West Country of England, is an early English lead glass *façon-de-Venise* wine, wheel engraved with the inscription 'God Save the Queen', plate 117, page 87. The short moulded stem is almost identical to one excavated in the City of London, which has a raven's head seal, the rebus of George Ravenscroft, applied to it.

In 1747 a popular marriage took place between Anne, daughter of George II, King of England, and William IV of Orange (not to be confused with King William III). A.C. has a pair of goblets, made to celebrate the event, one retaining its original lid, plate 120, page 89. One is engraved with her arms and the other with his. There is also a magnificent example in the Collection, probably engraved by Jacob Sang, which has the more usual combined coat of arms. These have lion and unicorn supporters and are sometimes mistaken for the royal coat of arms of Great Britain. This glass, plates 118 and 119, page 88, showing the back and front, proclaims the birth on March 8th 1748, of Willem Carel Hendrick Friso d'Fÿfde (William V of Orange and Nassau), son of the happy couple and destined to become, on his majority, the Stadhouder. It is beautifully inscribed, and engraved with a heraldic figure and various symbols. It is almost 8ins tall and once graced the famous Guepin Collection.

All the glasses I have mentioned above are wheel engraved, probably by Bohemian or Dutch specialists, either working abroad or in England. A stunning exception is the polychrome enamelled goblet which has already been glimpsed in this book, plate 87, page 71. It is purported to have been presented to William V when he reached his majority in 1766. Enamelled in brilliant colour with William's arms, it is signed 'Beilby Newcastle Pinxit'. A.C. is lucky enough to own this (doubly lucky, as I attempted to pass it through the plate glass door of a display cabinet while negotiating its purchase from Messrs. Delomosne & Sons at the Haughton's Ceramics Fair!). The glass belonged to the Nassau family until fairly recently, and is reputed to have been used at smart society gatherings for parlour games. Glasses of this size may sometimes be passed over by collectors as being too tall to go into their cabinets. I am glad to say that A.C. has no such reservations, his wife Penney has now to find other accommodation for some of her books! In fact, he has some great giant glasses, one of which will hold no less than two magnums. Some live in the cellar where they glint in the subdued light. I intend to borrow one for *the* dinner.

'Williamite' glasses are the subject of considerable controversy. Most are Irish and commemorate the Battle of the Boyne, where William finally defeated James in 1690. The glasses commemorating this event were made at various dates, but that's another story. A.C. has very good examples of the eighteenth century versions, plate 114, page 87.

*A.H.M.*

**Plate 113**, *page 85. Height 8⁵⁄₈ins.*

**Plate 114**, *page 85.  Heights 6⁷/₈ins, 7ins and 6⁷/₈ins.*

**Plate 115**, *page 85.  Height 2¹/₂ins.*

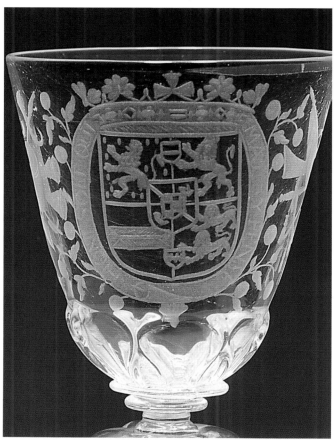

**Plate 116**, *page 85.  The reverse of plate 113.*

**Plate 117**,
*page 85.
Height 4ins.*

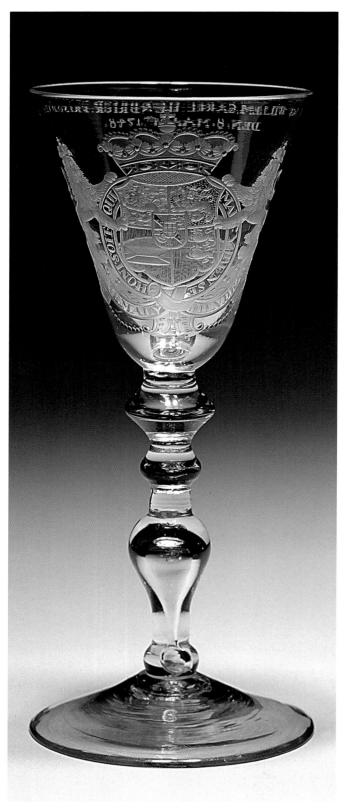

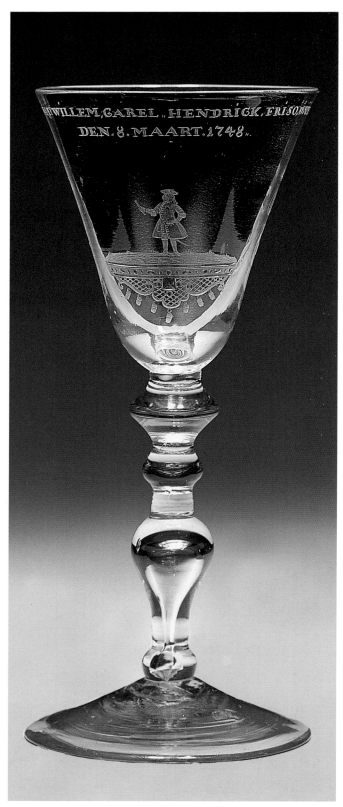

**Plate 118**, *page 85. Height 7³⁄₄ins.*

**Plate 119** *Reverse of plate 118.*

**Plate 120**, *page 85. Heights 7³/₄ins and 11ins with lid.*

# SQUARE STEMS FOR
# A SQUARE KING

The Hanoverian King George I, a stolid North German citizen not even much interested in Britain in spite of his English ancestors, totally lacked the romantic appeal of the Stuarts. The Jacobites obviously considered him a usurper but he was descended directly from the Protestant side of the Royal Family, and so assumed the throne in 1714, succeeding Queen Anne. (The later Stuarts, children of King James by his second marriage, had followed their fathers conversion to Roman Catholicism, and thus debarred themselves). This event was celebrated in glass with the introduction of a new stem type, the moulded pedestal. Initially these had four sides, and an occasional one also bore royal emblems. A very few of these still exist. The one in A.C.'s Collection has crowns moulded on the shoulders and stars on the sides, plates 121, 122 and 123.

Since the design was rarely seen in England before Hanoverian George, it is termed 'Silesian'. In extremely rare instances, the sides carry the words GOD SAVE THE KING or GOD SAVE KING GEO., one word to each side, but all seem to refer directly to his coronation. Later, the stem developed six, then eight sides and was largely abandoned from use on wine glasses and goblets by about 1740, but for some reason continued until the end of the century and later, to be used for candlesticks, tapersticks, sweetmeats and tazzae. As so often with glass design, its original adoption followed fashionable silver shapes, but branched off on a route of its own.

**Plate 121**  *Height 6ins.*

**Plate 122**,
*above and page 28.*

**Plate 123**, *above and page 28.*
*Height 6ins.*

# PUTTING A NAME ON IT

Glasses bearing designs – engraved, gilt or painted – relating to the consumption of beverages other than wine (the vine in one form or another) or ale (hops and barley) are not common. The few that there are will be decorated with apples for cider, or pears for the beverage perry (made in the same manner as cider from fermented pear juice). No change of design in the shape of the glass was attempted – it was left to the decorator to convey the intended use. Thus a facet ale glass could readily be converted for cider-drinking by engraving it with the appropriate fruit, plate 124. Outside the baluster and balustroid periods, glasses of different types were so treated, although an incised twist perry glass, shown here with an unusual similarly-stemmed, honeycomb moulded wine, is an extreme rarity. Note also the dimple moulding and folded foot on the perry glass, plate 125.

The two air twist glasses, plate 126, page 92 are also most interesting. The double-knopped one, though elegant, is of a fairly normal wine glass form. Its real focus of interest is the fruiting apple branches with which it is engraved. The other is even more unusual; it is a two-piece air twist with a bell bowl which displays an entire fruit tree.

Other glasses bear the word CIDER or, perhaps more commonly, CYDER. The spelling of PERRY does not, to my knowledge, vary. An unusual drink whose name appears on the bowls of glasses, mostly multi-spiral air twist drawn trumpets, is Capillaire, plate 127, page 92, illustrated here with a rare flute glass engraved with fruiting vine. Capillaire was a concoction based on orange-flower water and maidenhair fern, for which there are many recipes. Whether it was alcoholic or not is uncertain – the existence of these small glasses seems to imply that it was. Certainly, it was used as a sweetening agent for raw spirits, and Dr. Samuel Johnson (1709-84), who liked his liquor strong, was in the habit of adding it to port – which speaks worlds as to either the quality of contemporary port, or to that of Dr. J.'s palate.

Decanters are another matter. As we shall see, their contents could be named or their bodies otherwise decorated in a variety of styles.

**Plate 124**, *page 61. Heights 7¹/₄ins and 7ins.*

**Plate 125**, *page 34. Heights 6⁷/₈ins and 4¹/₂ins.*

**Plate 126**, *page 91.  Heights both 7¼ins.*

· **Plate 127**, *page 91.  Heights 7½ins and 5⅜ins.*

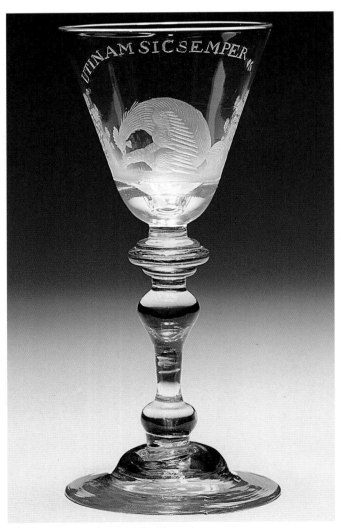

**Plate 128**, *opposite.  Height 7ins.*

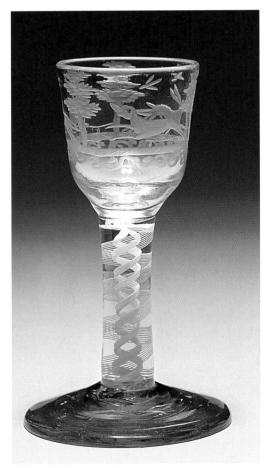

**Plate 129**, *opposite.  Height 4¾ins.*

**Plate 130**

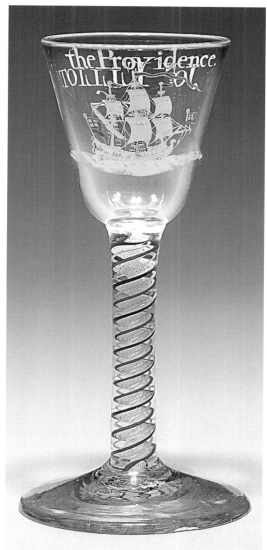

**Plate 131** *Height 6¼ins.*

## DECORATING FOR OTHER REASONS

Sporting subjects were often used, as for example on this nice ogee-bowled cotton twist, with its amusingly primitive coursing scene, plate 129, opposite.

Horse-racing, individual famous horses, hunting, and all manner of field sports and pastimes were used by engravers. One sometimes encounters glasses with obscure inscriptions or illustrations which may be political satire or even private jokes, but whose meanings have been lost. Of others, there are some recognised types, like this mating cock and hen glass, a fine Newcastle, plate 128 (opposite). This is a good example of the group, with engraving that is almost as crude as its subject. The meaning is fairly obvious. It would have been intended as a gift to a lady who had taken some

gentleman's fancy. Eighteenth century humour was frequently as broad as the girth of many a well-nourished, heavy-drinking squire. The dog Latin of the inscription is open to various suggestive translations.

## WISHING THEM LUCK

'SUCCESS TO...' glasses, engraved more usually than painted, were commissioned throughout the eighteenth century. They refer to specific towns, politicians seeking election, royalty and nobility, soldiers and seamen, and especially privateers – privately owned ships setting out to seek their owners' fortunes, in merchant ventures, the capture of enemy vessels in time of war or often straight-forward piracy. These maritime glasses usually carry both the name of the ship and her captain, and are often dated, plates 130 and 131.

Plate 132 *Heights 11¼ins and 5⅝ins.*

Plate 133 *Heights 6½ins and 6⅛ins.*

Plate 134 *Height 4¾ins.*

The PROVIDENCE and its master JOHN ELLIOT are most handsomely celebrated in this extremely rare Beilby interpretation of such a commission. The fact that they, the owners or 'Captain Elliot', chose additionally to use a rare (and presumably expensive), colour twist glass sets this apart as something truly special. The 1767 date is very helpful in dating other specimens of similar type and colouring. The stem is beautifully formed and the colour combination appears to be unique. The whole effect is a *tour-de-force* of English glassmaking and decorating.

Engraved privateer glasses date mainly from the second half of the eighteenth century and usually occur on cotton twist glasses. The facet cut 'Lord Clive' firing glass, two sides of which are shown, plate 134, is a great rarity. The right hand glass of plate 133 is also very unusual in that it has a simple bunch of grapes – no ship – with which to wish 'Success to the London'. John Knill's glass beside it is more traditional and stylish in design. A fine bucket bowl is engraved to depict the Eagle Frigate in full sail, obviously intent on SUCCESS. This is an outstanding specimen of a much sought, seldom found, glass type. I have already spoken on page 17 of 'ye Good Intent', plate 132, the matching glass and decanter. It is not likely that a discovery of such magnitude will re-occur. 'Jaˢ Brooks Captain' is also inscribed.

# TO SEA IN SHIPS

The eighteenth century English and Dutch tradition of having glassware, and in particular wine glasses, engraved with ships and shipping subjects seems strange at first glance. Surely these delicate, beautifully engraved (or even painted) Newcastles and their Dutch equivalents would not long have survived the rough-and-tumble conditions on board a tiny (by modern standards) unstable sailing ship, tossed like a leaf by oceanic waves as big as houses and like as not to founder or be attacked at any time. The answer of course is that they probably never went to sea at all, except perhaps for one or two 'specials', kept safe and securely cushioned in the captain's cabin, taken from their padded cases only for ceremonial use. Mostly they remained safe ashore in the ship owners' cabinets or displayed in the boardroom of some merchant venture company, such as the Verenigd Oost-indische Companie (United East-India Company), better known by its acronym VOC, the huge Dutch conglomerate that formerly controlled virtually all trade between Europe and the Dutch East Indies (now mostly Indonesia) Plates 135, 136, 137 and 139, page 96.

Plate 138 and plate 140, page 96 show another glass made for the trading companies. This Silesian stemmed goblet is engraved with the Dutch lion, on the globe, between two ships sailing in opposite directions, intent on DE NEGOTIE (trade). Over the stern of one ship is the letter O (for Oosten), over the other W (for the West Indian Company).

Seagoing glass is an entirely different matter. By the late eighteenth century we find some elegant decanters with very broad, spreading bases clearly designed for maximum stability and therefore ideal for use aboard ship, see plate 190, page 122. These and some glasses with exaggeratedly large, thick feet – much wider and heavier than even firing glasses – were the pieces especially made for use at sea.

But commoner glass, however unsuitable, was also brought aboard. Some was found amongst the famous salvage of the 'Geldermalsen' which sank in the East Indies in 1751. Along with the gold bars and fine Chinese porcelains recovered were domestic articles belonging to the crew, including what was probably the remains of the captain's glass (fragments of a beaded light baluster), three air twists, a balustroid gin, a salt cellar, and a ribbed tumbler – surprising finds all. Only the gin glass appears to be of English origin – possibly an export type. Alan Milford has been able to put together perfect examples of all the above glasses.

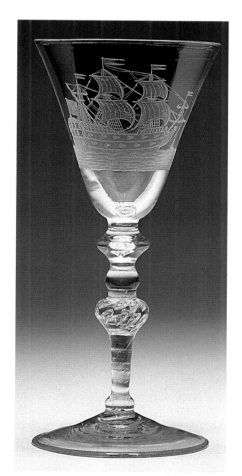

**Plate 135** *Height 7³/₄ins.*

**Plate 136** *The reverse of plate 135, Height 7³/₄ins.*

**Plate 137** *Close-up of plate 135.*

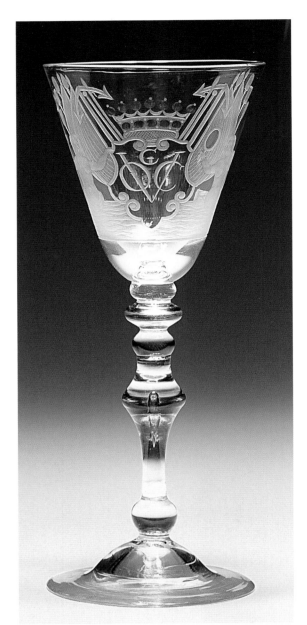

**Plate 138**, *page 95. Height 6³⁄₄ins.*

**Plate 139**, *page 95. Heigh 7³⁄₄ins.*

**Plate 140**, *close-up of plate 138.*

# BACCHUS

Throughout time, vessels in materials of all sorts were made and decorated specifically for the wine drinker. Here are a few glass specimens that A.C. has found. Surprisingly, only the air twist names 'Bacchus' as the sitter. The heaviest, a balustroid (perhaps Newcastle) glass, plate 141, has 'Hansie in de Kelder', a double entendre, intended for presentation to a pregnant lady. On the others, Bacchus sits on his barrel and enjoys his wine. The two Newcastle glasses on page 98 have much finer engraving.

**Plate 142**   *Height 6⁵⁄₈ins.*

**Plate 141**   *Height 7¹⁄₄ins.*

**Plate 143**   *Height 6¹⁄₂ins.*

**Plate 144,** *page 97.  Heights both 8ins.*

**Plate 145** *Heights 4⁵/₈ins and 6¹/₄ins.*

## BLOWING RASPBERRIES – PRUNTS

These blobs applied to English glass derive from seventeenth century Dutch and north German roemers, where their purpose was not decorative but rather preventative, stopping greasy – and often drunken – fingers from allowing the vessel to slither through their grasp. The 'raspberry' was not *really* blown, but formed of molten glass impressed onto the stem in the same manner as a seal is applied in wax on a document. In the late seventeenth, eighteenth and early nineteenth centuries, vast numbers of roemers were manufactured in Britain in green lead glass, mainly for export. Research in this field is now being done.

As you can readily see on these fine specimens of A.C.'s, plate 146, the base of the bowl has been formed into a fat cylinder, to which are applied four raspberry prunts, a most interesting design, here surely used solely as decoration. Rarest of all is this sophisticated design (in the centre) with its green ogee bowl and conical foot linked by a knopped single series twist stem. A.C.'s friend, Jay Kaplan has an even rarer glass with blue bowl and foot.

## UNUSUAL DECORATIVE DEVICES AND OTHER NOVELTIES
### Getting Your Thruppenceworth

Inserting a coin or token into a hollow spherical knop is a rare feature found in combination with several stem types – baluster, plain or even, as here on the right, a cotton twist, plate 145. The most usual introduction, perhaps, was a silver three-penny piece (colloquially 'thruppence') but many other medallions, such as the Dutch token here, and coins of low value are found. The low chalice has a George II Lima groat dated 1745.

Where such coins are dated, they must not be taken as reliable indicators of the age of the glasses concerned; they are almost always earlier in date, rarely contemporary. The most these coins can tell us is that they are never later than the glasses!

**Plate 146** *Heights 5¹/₂ins, 6ins and 6¹/₂ins.*

**Plate 147** *The yard of ale glass which A.C. bought from Dwight Lanmon was formerly the property of the famous conductor, Sir Thomas Beecham.*

## MEASURING THE MESS – YARDS AND HALF-YARDS OF ALE

These are elongated glass trumpets of approximately the specified length, with flared mouth and bulbous, usually spherical, bottom end. Most date from the nineteenth century, but examples from the baluster period are known. The bottom end of these latter is sometimes formed as a large acorn, as is the case with A.C.'s fine example, illustrated here, plate 147, once owned by Sir Thomas Beecham.

The amusement value of these glasses is well known. Tavern drinkers naive or rash enough to try, would – usually for a bet – endeavour to drink them dry, sometimes with the added impetus of doing so against the clock, without spilling any of their contents. This feat is a near impossibility, since as the long glass is tilted, air must eventually enter the bulb at the end, resulting in a rush of liquid into the face of the drinker – and the consequent hilarity of all other customers.

## THE PLEASURE OF RUINING YOUR GUESTS' CLOTHES – TRICK GLASSES

Fine drinking glasses were sometimes not quite what they seemed. Look at the engraved floral pattern below the lip of this pretty Newcastle from A.C.'s Collection, plate 149. The main illustration does not reveal the fact that two of the flowers on one side are centrally pierced. Look to the close-up, plate 148. The prankster could safely sip from the area he knew to be untampered with, which is marked with a tiny flower, then offer the glass to the chosen victim, knowing that they would almost certainly try to drink from the other side, with disastrous results. Even if the glass were simply set on the table with the holes facing the diner, the outcome would probably be the same. Such trick glasses were only real fun when filled with red wine, port or some other staining beverage. Such wines pouring onto an expensive Brussels lace cravat or fichu were certain to provoke howls of merriment from other guests, well worth the risk, even if the trick provoked a slap in the face – or even a challenge to a duel. This particular glass may well owe its survival to its being one of the few caught by the hoaxer when it was thrown at him! The other glass in the picture is an acorn knopped composite stemmed air twist with the very finest of deeply engraved and polished foliage and floral scrolls – this time, not tampered with.

**Plate 148** *Close-up of plate 149.*

**Plate 149** *Heights 7ins and 6⁷/₈ins.*

# WHAT DO YOU KEEP IT IN?

## Some Notes on the History of Bottles with NEIL WILLCOX'S Informed Observations on the A.C. Hubbard, Jr. Bottle Collection

Anyone interested in the history of wine will have noted the range of containers – from goatskins to fine cut-glass decanters – in which it may be found. Here, however, we concern ourselves with bottles, since they were used to hold wine from the early times of glassmaking. Especially from the late seventeenth century onwards, bottles can throw a great deal of light upon wine production and preservation, social history and drinking habits in Europe – specifically in Stuart and Hanoverian England. Though English bottles were well made, they were obviously mass produced, cheap, 'throw-away' articles. But they were very strong, and this coupled with large production and obvious disposability has resulted in the survival of more of them than of many more fragile glass artifacts, though the majority of the earlier bottles which survive have been retrieved from the ground where they have lain buried, and acids in the soil do affect glass, often resulting in an iridescent surface patina.

Prior to the development of suitably strong glass bottles, a wide variety of materials had been used for the storage and transportation of wine and other liquids – pottery, wood, metal, leather, etc. By the late sixteenth century the stout stoneware quart bottle produced by German potters had become the standard on the European continent, in Britain and in her colonies – handled baluster form flagons, traditionally with a bearded face mask to the neck and an applied medallion on the body, commonly termed the Bellarmine bottle – a term said to derive from a fat, unpopular cardinal of that name, which it was supposed to resemble. The process of making this pottery – high fired and salt glazed to ensure it being impervious to liquids – was a trade secret. English potters had attempted to compete with it, to overcome being reliant on the importation of such a standard, everyday product. Aside from the considerable expense, the interruption of trade due to war was a major inconvenience. However, English potters were unable to achieve a competitive product until later in the seventeenth century, leaving the field open for the glass industry to exploit.

The basic bottle shape is comparatively easy to blow, but early specimens were thin-walled and until post medieval times brought improved design, were not usually considered suitable for transporting liquids like wine. After the breakup of the Roman Empire, roads had deteriorated and travel become much more difficult. Large bottles, when used, were packed in wooden boxes or baskets. These bottles were frequently square in section, but whatever the shape, they would have needed protecting with straw or other jacket material. It was a new concept to attempt to create from glass a product that could replace German stoneware – one that could withstand similar treatment in everyday use, bumpy roads, storage, shipping etc. What was required – and eventually produced – was a simple blown globular shape, with a neck by which to handle it, a mouth suitable for plugging with a stopper or cork, and a raised ring near the top of the neck – the 'string-ring' – to help in tying this down.

It was not until the 1670s – around the same time as George Ravenscroft's development of lead glass – that John Dwight of Fulham finally mastered the process fully and Britain was able to produce its own stoneware bottles, plate 150, page 102. Ironically this was achieved just when the bottle glasshouses had become so established that their product had finally reached parity in price with that of the imported stoneware article. The competition which the glass bottle had been presenting to the German Bellarmine can be seen in the increasingly poor quality of the latter from the 1650s onwards, with ever-decreasing attention being paid to detail by the potters, bearded face mask and medallion often becoming sketchy or disappearing completely. By the end of the century the market for the Bellarmine was over, and the glass bottle was firmly established as the vessel for common commercial packaging of liquids, launched on the path which still continues today.

At first, 'shaft-and-globe' shaped bottles seemed the obvious solution to the problem of creating a suitable glass wine container. A similar design (though thin walled) had been made in the Low Countries since the 1500s, plain or with an applied foot. This first design with an unstable, rounded base and long vulnerable neck, evolved in the 1670s and 1680s into a more rational form with a shorter neck and a broad, squat body – much steadier, more compact and practical. Impurities

**Plate 150**, *page 101. A good example, circa 1680, of the first commerical stoneware production achieved in England. Such quart sized handled flagons had been long mass-produced by potteries in Germany for export. John Dwight was finally able to challenge that monoply. Not only had Dwight been able to achieve the correct factors involved, such as clay type, high firing temperature and the technique of salt-glazing, he also manufactured a product of extremely high quality craftsmanship. The earlier German products were also of a high standard, but after the mid seventeenth century had deteriorated greatly. This flagon is typical of the high quality of English products of the time. Despite being a standard, everyday item, there is elegance of form and attention to detail. The ear-shaped handle is a distinctive characteristic of early English ceramic products.*

occurring naturally in the basic ingredient sand, gave bottle-glass its familiar dark green or greenish brown colour. It seems to have been wholly fortuitous that the cheapest 'metal' (as raw glass is known) also protected a bottle's contents from any injurious effects of light. Thus the glass bottle became a reliable, sturdy, cheap alternative to stoneware. Home produced, it was totally impermeable to the liquid contents, easier to clean for refilling, and could be recycled – glass cullet (broken or waste glass) lowered the cost of preparing a batch of glass and improved its quality when used in reasonably small quantities. So it was in considerable demand by glasshouses. Evolution of form continued gradually into the nineteenth century, and was remarkably consistent throughout all British glasshouses – allowing close dating

of surviving bottles by body form, style of string-ring etc.

Roman glass wine bottles had been wax sealed and opening them must have presented some difficulty. Later bottles and flasks were plugged with wood or hide, often waxed to ease withdrawal. Cork came into use in the seventeenth century, but as with its predecessors had to be left standing proud of the neck, in the manner of the modern champagne or sparkling wine cork, in order that it could be pulled. The 'string-ring' had an evolution all of its own, from broad disc to blade-shape in section, to a blunt wedge shape, to forming an integral part of the bottle mouth and thence to the vestigal remains one finds today. With the invention of the corkscrew, originally called 'bottle-screw' in about 1680, it became possible to insert the cork flush with the top of the bottle. One notes that early bottles with broken necks (their corks still tied down) are found, especially on excavations of military camps and forts in the West Indies. Speculation arises as to whether such damage was sometimes deliberately caused – frustration at being unable to draw the cork, or on breaking it – since even in our technological age a wholly satisfactory method of pulling corks has yet to be devised, and most of us have experienced the annoyance of the broken or jammed cork. In the seventeenth and eighteenth centuries, smashing off the neck of a wine bottle was occasionally practised as a speedy way of getting at the contents.

# SETTING THE SEAL ON IT
# WINE AND THE GLASS BOTTLE

In the seventeenth and eighteenth centuries, wine was generally imported in casks. For all but the largest and most wealthy households, the practice had been to have one's bottles filled at the vintner or obtained as needed

**Fig. 33** *Trade cards and billheads offer an interesting insight into the bottle trade – Janson & Popplewell's pretty, modest little advertisement shows some naive bottle shapes. Clearly these were made in Newcastle, and shipped to London with the coal their firm also sold – not an unusual combination of trade at this time.* © *Copyright The British Museum.*

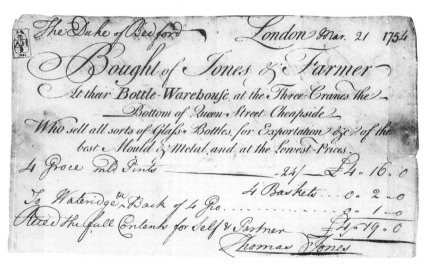

**Fig. 34** *The John Webb invoice mentions 'bottles for exportation of the best mould and metal', blown moulded bottles would standardise size and ensure accurate pint and quart capacities. © Copyright The British Museum.*

**Fig. 35** *The basket was the main container in which to transport bottles, and the term 'Wateridge' suggests that the favoured method of transport was by barge, the obvious alternative to pack animals or carts once waterways and canals became widely available. © Copyright The British Museum.*

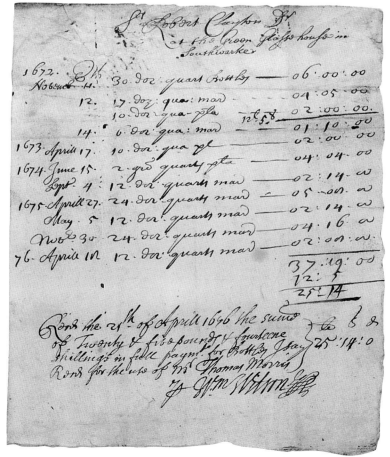

**Fig. 36** *A very interesting seventeenth century bottle invoice from the glasshouse of Thomas Morris in Southwark (a borough of London). By 1672 a quart standard of size had been established. Some idea of the alcohol consumption of the day can be imagined by adding up the number of bottles supplied (but not fully paid for) to a gentleman like Sir Robert over a four-year period – in excess of two thousand, two hundred bottles. These would have been re-used, since at the time wine was normally laid down in the barrel and only bottled as required. Had the date been later, the number of bottles required by Sir Robert might have been considerably more, as he was Lord Mayor of London in 1679. © Copyright The British Museum.*

from a tavern which – as opposed to the more common alehouse – had exclusive rights to retail wine.

The fashion of placing a moulded 'medallion' on the body of the imported stoneware bottle no doubt influenced the similar practice of applying a glass seal during the bottle production. Soon after the glass bottle was introduced, the usefulness became apparent of having bottles marked with an identifying seal. The fact that this form of permanent 'label' could be added simply and at little extra cost, that it was available locally and on a short-order basis, and that it could be altered simply with each order, gave the fledgling glass bottle industry the edge which it needed in the early days while its product was considerably more expensive than the imported stoneware competition. This was of particular relevance for taverns, ensuring the return of their containers when wine was ordered. A high proportion of sealed bottles which survive from the seventeenth century are marked for specific taverns. They generally used a pictorial symbol as on their inn signs, together with the initials of the licensee (and often of his wife also). These can sometimes be identified from records of tenancy and can help in the dating of such bottles where the seal itself is not dated.

For private customers, an applied seal identified their bottles with the particular wine they had ordered. Such customers used a seal bearing their crest or coat of arms and/or their initials or full name. By the end of the seventeenth century, fewer tavern seals are encountered and most bear details of private individuals. Happily for the historian or collector today, by the start of the eighteenth century it had become an established fashion to order one's own marked bottles. No doubt, there was an element of social status as well as practical reasons for this. The fashion continued well into the 1820s, and well over a thousand different seals are recorded, many surviving only as detached seals from broken bottles but nevertheless often providing a fascinating direct and traceable link to individuals in the past.

Although an increasing number of seals were dated, it is not clear why – with few exceptions – such dates appear to indicate when the bottle was made, rather than the vintage of the wine it contained or when it was bottled.

## PUTTING A CORK IN IT

As wine drinking increased and cork came into use as a stopper, it was found that wine could, with advantage, be allowed to age in the bottle. It had become a practical reality to store bottles on their sides, so that the liquid remained in contact with the cork, preventing this from drying out. The Methuen Treaty of 1703 was responsible for promoting a large increase in the consumption of port, which required aging in the bottle. The globular body of earlier wine bottles was becoming impractical and a straight-sided form was developing, evolving towards the standard cylindrical shape of today.

## POURING WITH ELEGANCE
## SERVING BOTTLES

It was not until the 1730s-40s that the clear glass decanter came into widespread use – the glass bottle being very much a serving vessel as well as one for storage of wine. Although mass produced, the English wine bottle was hand crafted, with attention to detail, and especially when adorned with a seal would have presented itself well at the table. Nevertheless, from the start it was probably regarded as a cheap, commonplace container – in the end disposable. Added to this were the facts that the forms soon became old-fashioned, that the material was liable to be damaged by casual use, that it could be recycled... these all contributed to the comparative rarity of good examples. Consequently, for the earliest and rarest bottles the collector is often dependent on excavated items – those which have survived total destruction, and which are now historical artifacts as much as early specimens of glassmaking.

Early wine bottles with applied handles are rare survivors – eminently useful, functional and inexpensive, factors that have no doubt guaranteed that this should be the case. That handles were far from rare at the time is evinced by their inclusion as a standard extra in an early price list.

Unlike lead glass (so-called 'crystal' products) bottle glass tended to be treated in a rough and ready manner – the more useful the object, the more likely it was to continue in use until broken. The fact that they sometimes bore interesting seals, of family or historical interest, has ensured the survival of many wine bottles bearing these. That their forms would soon seem quaint and old-fashioned perhaps also assisted in their survival.

A.C.'s bottles have been very carefully selected, not only in order to be as representative of their period as possible and to illustrate the sequential progression of their shapes (invaluable to archeologists in dating such things as shipwrecks, early building sites and waste dumps), but also to show them properly as stylish artifacts in their own right. The Collection also contains a high proportion of extreme rarities, several examples probably being unique.

**Plate 151**  *Dating from around the middle of the seventeenth century, this little bottle, 7½ins, was found awhile back, in the roots of a fallen oak tree, in a field near Shrewsbury. It is a small size 'shaft-and-globe', carrying the initials 'E' incorporated with the letter 'T', plus a 'B'. These are probably the initials of the owner and his wife, the first conjoined letters covering their separate Christian names, the last, their shared surname.*

*Although early examples such as this bearing seals are very rare, the specialised bottle collector has an advantage in that there is always the possibility that others may be literally unearthed... accidental finds, construction sites in cities... there is always the chance that important new discoveries will be made. This very special example is a particularly significant discovery, an unrecorded seal, a bottle of scarce half size, and also in exceptional condition for one recovered from the ground.*

**Plate 152** *Four examples of the classic 'shaft-and-globe' type which come from the important opening epoch of the English glass wine bottle: 1630-1665. Left to right: an iridescent circa 1650 crested bottle which belonged to the Earl of Wemyss and bears his swan, surmounting the coronet, on the seal (see also plate 154); a somewhat longer necked 1660s 'tavern bottle' having the landlord's name 'William Cliffton' and the sign of the Fleece in London's Covent Garden (see also plate 153); an even taller 1650s type bearing a seal design of a stag facing sinister, and initials, S.N. (again, probably a tavern piece); and one of the armorial bottles from the cellars of William Breck of Upton (1622-1663), whose name it carries. He married Elisabeth, daughter of Sir Robert Berewood of Chester, Kent (one time King's Bench judge). This is a half size example of 7¼ins high.*

*The Fleece enjoyed an unsavoury reputation, as Samuel Pepys records thus:*

*1 December 1660*

*'Mr Shaply and I went into London, and calling upon Mr Pinkny the Goldsmith, he took us to the tavern and gave us a pint a wine, and there fell into our company old Mr Flower and other gentleman, who did tell us how a Scotch Knight was killed basely the other day at the Fleece in Covent-garden, where there hath been a great many formerly killed'.*

*25 November 1661*

*'Went to the opera and saw the last act of Bondman, and there find Mr Sanchy and Mrs Mary Archer, sister to the fair Betty, whom I did admire at Cambridge. And then we took them to the fleece in Covent Garden, there to bid goodnight to Sir W. Penn, who stayed for me. But Mr Sanchy could not by any argument get his lady to trust herself with him into the taverne which he was much troubled at, and so we returned immediately into the city by Coach, and at the Miter in Cheapside there light and drank, and then set her at her uncles in the Old Jury'.*

*Aubrey also reports of the Fleece that it: "...was very unfortunate for homicides, there have been several killed – three in my time. It is now (1692) a private house. Clifton the master hanged himself, having perjured himself".*

*William Clifton, tavern keeper 1651-1675 issued tokens as:*
*Obv: AT THE FLEECE TAVERNE (A fleece) (1/4d)*
*Rev: IN COVENT GARDEN encircling W.C.,*
*Obv: WILLIAM CLIFTON AT THE (A fleece) (1/2d)*
*Rev: FLEECE IN COVENT GARDEN encircling W.C.*

*The tavern was situate in Bridge Street on a site now occupied by the Drury Lane theatre. The Rose tavern, close to the Fleece, also had a reputation as a notorious haunt of gamblers and rufflers, which gives some indication that this whole area was not of the highest public standard, hence the reluctance on the part of ladies to enter, even with a male escort.*

*Literature: English Inn Signs by Jacob Larwood and John Camden Hotten (1951), BBR 77 April/June 1998, S&G.*

**Plate 153**

**Plate 154**

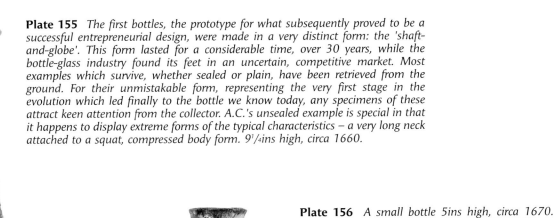

**Plate 155** *The first bottles, the prototype for what subsequently proved to be a successful entrepreneurial design, were made in a very distinct form: the 'shaft-and-globe'. This form lasted for a considerable time, over 30 years, while the bottle-glass industry found its feet in an uncertain, competitive market. Most examples which survive, whether sealed or plain, have been retrieved from the ground. For their unmistakable form, representing the very first stage in the evolution which led finally to the bottle we know today, any specimens of these attract keen attention from the collector. A.C.'s unsealed example is special in that it happens to display extreme forms of the typical characteristics – a very long neck attached to a squat, compressed body form. 9¹/₄ins high, circa 1660.*

**Plate 156** *A small bottle 5ins high, circa 1670. This displays similar characteristics to plate 155 but shows the beginning of a rationalisation from the old fashioned 'shaft-and-globe' form towards a more stable, compact, 'onion' shape. Within a fairly short period, from the 1670s to the 1680s, this transition was complete and the basic 'onion' which followed became the standard product for over 30 years, well into the 1720s, when the 'mallet' evolved.*

**Plate 158** *A 1670s bottle of transitional form, showing well the midway period during which the design was being re-evaluated, between the 'shaft-and-globe' and 'onion' contours. The seal bears a 'Fleur-de-Lys' framed by fronds. This was in fact a commonly used crest at the time, and without further clues, such as a motto or surname, or provenance tying it to a particular source, it is impossible to attribute it to an original owner.*

**Plate 157** *'C P 1697' sealed bottle of half size. A minority of sealed bottles bear dates – those which do are inevitably of greater interest to the collector. Seventeenth century dated examples are particularly rare and sought after. This example, aside from its early date and rare size, is also one of those which have survived the years above ground without being discarded and interred as are so many of its fellows. Whether kept in a cellar, discovered in the thatch of a roof or actually handed down through generations as a keepsake, these early bottles in 'cellar found' condition are rare.*

**Plate 159** *Six bottles, spanning the period from the 1660s to the 1730s, which represent the exceptions that occur, in colour or in size. All are out of the ordinary. The standard size 'onion' in the middle of the back row displays well a rare feature which can appear in early blown black glass bottles during production. An excess of naturally occurring sodium sulphate in the molten glass floats to the surface. If the glass blower takes his 'gather' (the amount of molten glass required from which to blow the bottle) from this, rather than clearing this layer to reach the cleaner mix beneath, the final product will show a distinctive opaque turquoise blue surface colour. Held up to the light, such bottles still appear standard olive green.*

**Plate 160** *A pair of large sized, double magnum bottles from the last quarter of the seventeenth century. Variations from the standard quart capacity are considerable rarities. That on the left is of a typical early eighteenth century shape; the one to the right has the lower set string ring, more acutely tapered neck configuration and the more bucket-shaped body of a decade or so before, circa 1690. A.C. also has a circa 1675 magnum form in excellent condition, a very rare item.*

**Plate 161** *A circa 1700 black glass 'onion' with armorial seal. The original owner has not yet been determined. Researching the background to certain bottles and trying to attribute them to a specific individual or family whose arms or initials are shown on the seal is part of the appeal of these artifacts.*

109

**Plate 162** *While handled versions of the standard early bottles are very rare survivors, it is interesting to observe in an early bottle price list advertisement that handles were offered as a standard extra. A handled 'shaft-and-globe' is known and a few 'onion' forms with such handles are recorded. These date to the period before the clear lead glass table decanter had started to become a standard product. Wine had been stored in barrels and the bottle served as receptacle and table dispenser prior to decanting. By the 1730s, clear decanters had begun to take the place of bottles on the table. The latest example of handled bottles shown here, lacking a string ring and with a pouring spout, is in fact more rarely encountered than the earlier version of circa 1720 on the left. The footed, handled mug in the centre and as plate 163 (termed a 'gorge' in early ceramic sales lists) is a form found in stoneware, silver and clear or 'milk' glass in the late seventeenth and early eighteenth centuries. This is an example of a rare one-off production, not a standard item – a unique survivor of absolute museum quality. There are a handful of roughly comparable double sealed or otherwise unusually embellished items known in ordinary bottle glass from this early period. The handles all bear a thumb-piece at the top and are eminently practical to use. This, ironically, is probably the very reason for their extreme rarity today; little valued in their time, they were used to destruction. This well illustrates an important aspect of appreciating today these commonplace items of centuries ago. The higher rated, such as silver and gold, were more likely to be valued and to survive.*

**Plate 163** *The footed mug, as above, showing the seal.*

**Plate 164** *Above, four good examples of bottles typical of the period 1718 to circa 1750. Left to right: 'I Tweed 1720', a broad bodied form, wider than it is tall, termed a 'pancake onion'; an extraordinary circa 1750 squat bodied 'mallet', intriguingly marked on the seal 'EARLE OF LITCHFEILD STOLE IF SOLD. The 'Augustine Earle Esq. 1729' is of an early, compressed body mallet form. The owner's home was Heydon Hall, Norfolk, built in the 1580s. The seal is in a particularly pleasing elaborate script. Unlike today in Britain, the title 'esquire' was then strictly applied only to gentlemen of coat armour, i.e. titled. The smallest bottle is a half sized 'onion' sealed 'Uric 1718'. In attempting to research such seals, one should bear in mind* that at these dates, spelling was still phonetic and not formalised. Also, many artisans were illiterate, so misspellings like 'Litchfeild' abound. George Henry Lee, the third Earl, succeeded to the title in 1743 and was a Chancellor of Oxford University until his death in 1772. There was insufficient glass on the seal of the Litchfield bottle for the Earl's coronet to be clearly shown – but the bottle was obviously owned by the Earl (an ancestor of Patrick Litchfield, the photographer). This 9½ins high bottle is also unique for its period by virtue of the fact that it carries on the seal a warning about possible theft. A message in the bottle, no less!*

**Plate 165** *A unique assemblage of Oxford (and one Cambridge) sealed wine bottles. It contains several very rare and noteworthy specimens. Back row, left to right: dark red-amber cylindrical form with seal marked 'Mag.Co.C.R.', 1769 (Magdalen College Common Room); a stunning contrast in terms of the variation of colour one may encounter in the products of different glasshouses at the time, is the filled-with-air-bubbles green cylinder with seal, 'All Souls College 1764'; a dark olive cylinder sealed 'Emmanuel College' (from the only Cambridge college whose sealed bottles survive); a squatter, dark olive cylinder with seal marked 'Ch.Ch.C.R. 1801' (Christ Church Common Room), a previously unrecorded dated example from this college; a very early example of the cylinder form, circa 1740, and the only such known to survive, sealed 'St.I.C.R. Oxon' (St. John's Common Room).*
*Front row, left to right: an 'onion' dated 1689 from the Crown tavern*

*– while many dated seals are known for various years between 1683 and 1701 from this tavern, this example has not previously been recorded; olive green 'mallet' form of circa 1740, from Jesus College, marked 'I C C R'; and a dark glass 'onion' dated 1707, again from the Crown tavern. The Jesus College 'mallet' is the only known sealed college bottle of this shape and date. The city of Oxford plays a particularly relevant part in the history of the sealed wine bottle in England. Not only has it left a greater legacy in terms of the quantity and variety of types from the earliest times than any city other than London, but it was also the first to have these artifacts studied. From the early twentieth century, and still to this day, the seventeenth and eighteenth century college and tavern bottles of Oxford continue to benefit from much in-depth research. The bottles in the front row are also illustrated below.*

**Plate 166**

**Plate 167**

**Plate 168**

**Plate 169** *The curiously shaped, rarely encountered sealed 'bladders' form a group of free blown wine bottles which appeared after the 'onions' and saw use alongside the more familiar binnable early straight sided types.*

*Left to right:, a most unusual 1760s form with its seal marked 'Holt Mineral Water, Wilts'; a much smaller bottle with seal marked 'In. Hawkins, 1741'; an example of the rarer style of 'bladder', more correctly, perhaps, described as a 'side-flattened onion', with a seal to*

*one narrow end marked 'Matthew Jofe, 1725'; and one of A.C.'s favourites, a half size type marked on its seal 'P Baftard, 1725'. The West Country Bastard family are known to have favoured this sort of bottle in the second and third quarters of the eighteenth century.*

*The 'Bastard' sealed bottle illustrates a point: while well crafted, early English bottles were free blown, one-off items and therefore exhibit individuality of character; the asymmetrical form of this particular example enhances its attraction to the modern eye.*

**Plate 170** *Distinctive bottles probably shipped to America from England. A very rare and significant 9½ins example of circa 1760 with the seal wording 'Old Colony 1620'. This was obviously made to commemorate the Mayflower pilgrims' journey to the New World and is particularly interesting. Although there are many contemporary American accounts and advertisements in the period from about 1730 onwards relating to the availability of locally produced bottles (including sealed ones in the English manner), not a single well-documented example survives. Such eighteenth century seals as have been excavated in Williamsburg and elsewhere, made for known colonists, have every appearance of having been ordered from British glasshouses, as indeed do these two bottles. 'Old Colony 1620' definitely dates from the period before the American Revolution. This 11ins plus (with silver neck mount), squat-bodied cylindrical type, marked on seal 'Sidney Breese, 1765' bottle is one of about four known. The original owner, Sidney Breese (1709-1767) was a Welshman who settled in New York City in 1730. He was a merchant who imported English goods such as looking-glasses and fabrics for resale.*

**Plate 171** *Even unsealed, such octagonal forms as these are rare: the earliest dated example, which is in the Collection, is from 1731; it is blown in a dip mould and is flat sided rather than globular as were the immediately preceding 'onion' forms. Such bottles answered the problem of standardising capacity as well as of suitability for binning.*

*Left to right: a black glass, long necked, octagonal bodied type with seal marked '(G)R.S.173(9)' (although bottle seals were carefully stamped with the metal 'die' it is not uncommon for the applied 'blob' of glass to have been rather smaller than needed and, as in this case, the full information does not appear. A few other examples of this seal exist so we know of the first initial and the full date); a little 6½ins unsealed simpler piece; a black glass, long necked, rectangular bodied variety (with flattening of corner edges), the seal marked 'Foote, Harwood, 1731'; this bottle is A.C.'s absolute favourite. Although the seal (placed on the broad face) bears the same date as appears on the other octagonal example here ('PM/1731', sealed on the narrow face), their date of manufacture is in fact some forty years apart. The 'PM/1731' is almost certainly of that date – the string rim conforms well to that period, and there is no reason to question this bottle's date. This is in fact a bottle of some considerable importance, bearing as it does the earliest date known on a bottle of this distinctive body form. The 'Foote, Harwood' bottle however displays all the characteristics of a bottle made around 1770, in particular the style of string ring. A very attractive bottle, this is an exception to the rule that the date on a seal is almost always that of manufacture of the bottle. John Pearson Foote of Harwood Manor, near Calstock, Cornwall, was in the process of constructing that Manor in 1731 – possibly the reason for choosing this as a commemorative date; finally, a lovely green glass similar body form, with a seal marked 'P.M.1731' affixed to one narrow edge of the bottle. These two bottles are shown individually in plates 172 and 173.*

**Plate 172**

**Plate 173**

113

**Plate 174** *The line-up demonstrates how diverse cylindrical bottles can be in height and capacity. There are no standard sizes here: a massive 12½ins double magnum with seal marked 'I.W.1772' towers over the half size 'Ed. Walters Pitcot, 1760', a rare quarter size '1791', and an exceptionally diminutive 'T. Thomas', 1789. Size is what counts here. Very large or especially small examples are difficult to come by. Bottles less than half size, themselves unusual, are exceptionally rare.*

**Figs. 37 and 38** *Today we rely on disposable packaging, but in the eighteenth and early nineteenth centuries the glass bottle was relatively expensive and reusable. You would take your own bottle to the wine merchant to refill. From this merchant's list, on the right, one recognises drinks such as MOUNTAIN and SHRUB that we find inscribed on Georgian decanters and wine labels. Guildhall Library, Corporation of London.*

**Plate 175** *'Thos. Rich – Over Stowey – 1783' Height 14ins. An example of the largest size of cylindrical bottle which was produced. This double magnum capacity is uncommon and extremely impressive, a particularly pleasing, well-proportioned example. Seals bearing a place name (in this case a village in Somerset) as well as the owner's full name and the date, are especially desirable today, allowing the best chance of research into the individual and his position in the local community. At the other extreme, the quarter bottle 'T. Thomas 1789', a mere 6¾ins by 3ins diameter, is of a size very rarely encountered.*

**Plate 176** *A stocky-bodied sealed bottle still carrying a paper label for 1806 imported madeira. Unusual in that it held this particular fortified wine (rather than port), and also because it is difficult to find labelled examples of any bottles from this period.*

**Plate 177** *A specially commissioned late eighteenth century wine bottle with a huge oval-shape applied seal. The seal bears a wealth of detail: the talbot's head on a wreath crest of the Malveysins, the Latin motto 'Juxta Salopian', and the date 1791.*

*The Malveysin family had long-established roots in Shropshire. Walter Malveysin came over with William the Conqueror, who granted him the manor of Malveysin Berwick in that county. Several of these bottles are known. For an individual, bottle seals allowed much scope for personal expression – surprisingly, this is an example of one of the few such 'expressions'. It is unique in the history of bottle seals in its size – it was purposely designed to be dramatic.*

115

**Plate 178** *The huge globular vessel and the stocky-bodied cylindrical type are both sealed 'H. ELLIS 1780'. At this period, the cylindrical body had become the standard for home use, the globular form appears only in exceptionally large bottles such as the first example. Although other giant sealed bottles of this kind are known, this pairing is unique in my experience for the use of identical seals on different forms.*

# HAD TO HAVES

**Plate 179** *The first is a 1770s straight sided bottle with the seal marked 'A.C.'; the second, a Ricketts-made, three-part moulded example of the 1820s, sealed 'I. Hubbard', the only Ricketts piece in the Collection. These two bottles were obviously destined to end up in A.C.'s Collection. Both were unknown and unrecorded before I knew of A.C. It was sheer chance that they appeared at a time when I was helping him to form this Collection.* N.W.

**Plate 180** *One other piece of glass – a late Georgian tumbler – appears in the Collection for the same sentimental reasons – it bears an engraving of a sportsman with a gun and his dog, and also the initials A.C. It is 5ins tall.*

**Plate 181** *A particularly fine Nailsea-type globular bottle, the seal marked 'S.W. 1792' – a unique piece with a particularly early date. In fact, I am unaware of another Nailsea-type decorated bottle bearing a seal dated in the eighteenth century. John Robert Lucas set up his Nailsea glassworks, south of Bristol, in 1788, so this bottle is one of the earlier pieces produced there. The glassworks closed in 1873. The bottles produced at Nailsea do not conform to the standard evolution of shape followed by other glasshouses, out-of-sequence globular and club decanter forms appear, plus the inclusion of white enamel splashes or pincered 'rigaree' trails.*

**Plate 182** *A beautifully formed, rare small, 6¼ins cylindrical bottle decanter, probably made at Alloa in the early nineteenth century. Again we have the applied pincered trailings (five rows on this one) on the bottle's sides. These aided grip as well as being decorative.*

**Plate 183** *Plenty of decorative white specks and splashes in the olive green to black glass again – but this time we are viewing the distinctive bottles of the north-of-the-border Alloa glassworks. Pictured: the cylindrical decanter bottles with applied pincered trailing to the sides, one with the seal 'J.B. 1828'; its companion with 'A.Y.1821', and symbols – probably identifying A.Y. as a tailor; and a miniature unsealed handled flagon. Note the variety of mouth finish. The majority of such Alloa sealed decanter bottles bear dates in the 1820s. Similar to the output of the Nailsea glassworks, the forms produced are separate from the standard evolutionary British wine bottle designs. Globular or club decanter styles predominate, lip shapes conform to the prevailing fashion.*

**Plate 184** *Varying in capacity, these seven bottles illustrate in chronological order the basic forms as they evolved from the first to the last decades of the eighteenth century.*

**Plate 185** *Here we come to the end of the story. A fine French assortment which would have held some splendid wines from the nineteenth century. The bottle in the centre of the front row is a rare English-made example from about 1830. While a few port bottles, etc., retain the use of a residual 'seal' in resin, or moulded in the glass, such 'Châteaux seals' represent the final chapter of commercial use of applied seals to blown bottles. Inevitably these nineteenth century seals are found on 'premier cru' wines, as recognisable back then as now: Château Lafitte, Margaux, Pichon Longueville... Late as these are, relative to the preceeding antique bottles, many are still rare survivors of containers from which the contents have been drunk. In one sense they are artifacts in their own right. In another, perhaps more romantic way, they are witness to an era, a time when promised quality was what was delivered. These examples of the last applied seals are a badge of honour. They are a mark of quality, surviving only as a (perhaps, elitist) reminder of that element.*

# OUT OF THE BOTTLE
## DECANTERS AND CLARET JUGS

Decanters evolved naturally from serving bottles. The early version of the claret jug appearing on the dining table was simply an 'onion' bottle, made in standard bottle glass, but with an applied handle to facilitate pouring. It is unlikely that wine was decanted in the modern sense of pouring it carefully from bottle to decanter. Rather, these serving bottles were simply filled from the barrel as required.

A curious type of decanter appeared early in the eighteenth century, the cruciform, which as its name implies was cross shaped in section. It had a moulded body, and a long, plain neck. It was made of clear lead glass, thick and heavily striated from the mould. Strangely, these moulds were not standardised, and so the bottles come in irregular sizes, usually surprisingly small. It would appear that the shape was designed to expose as much surface as possible to the ice or iced water in which they were presumably immersed. It follows that they were intended for chilling white wine. Another early decanter is the 'shaft and globe', which – except for the fact that it, too, is made of clear glass – duplicates in shape the seventeenth century bottle of the same name. These are usually depicted as having a ball-shaped, loose fitting stopper, the ball full of decorative tears. These stoppers may also be ground in, to fit snugly, as with contemporary medicine bottles, plate 192, page 123.

Shortly after, two shapes evolved almost simultaneously – the shoulder and the mallet. The first is rarer in normal size, but for some reason, commoner in the magnum and giant sizes, which are often engraved with labels naming their contents, and perhaps also with some fruiting vine or (in the case of ALE or BEER) hops and barley. The shape is self-descriptive, it being wider at the shoulder than the base. The correct stopper is a spire, cut with flat facets. The mallet – a misnomer frequently applied to the later Prussian-bodied type – takes its name from the sculptor's or stone-mason's mallet, which it resembles when held upside down, being wider at the base than the shoulder. At first, both these styles were quite plain, and the earliest decoration seems to have been applied only to the stoppers, as on the spire already mentioned. Early mallet stoppers were disc-shaped, flat and faceted at the edges. As cutting started to appear on the bodies of these decanters, so too the decoration of the stoppers became more elaborate and continued to evolve until being replaced by the mushroom type of the late eighteenth and early nineteenth century.

**Plate 186** *From the Collection, an early eighteenth century brass snuff box, signed F. Baker and made for The Lumber Troup, a drinking club. It is 3½ins long.*

# OF CANDLESTICKS AND KINGS
## and decanters too

The Wonderland of the Hubbard Collection contains other splendid things as well as drinking glasses – candlesticks, for example, with their strong cellar connections (candlelight and wine go together, like romance) and the velvety variations of colour in wine seen against candlelight is unforgettable. It is also highly informative to the oenophile.

more primitive types, possibly intended for cellar use. But the most sophisticated pieces shown here are the candlesticks and smaller taperstick of plate 188 and 189 (opposite). The smaller ones were made for daintier candles, and might well have graced a lady's tea tray with their elegantly slender twist stems and shining air beaded knops. But pride of place must surely be given to the

**Plate 187** *Heights both 6ins.*

Naturally A.C. has several candlesticks, often matching in their stem construction the finest work on contemporary wine glasses. Plate 13, page 29, shows an excellent baluster type (with candle) between two magnificent acorn knopped glasses of the same period. These two small candlesticks in plate 187 are interesting,

candlestick in plate 189, from the collection of the late Tony Stout. Its gadrooned inverted saucer foot is unique in my experience and the tapering twist construction of its stem works superbly – masterpiece of illuminating accessory that it is.

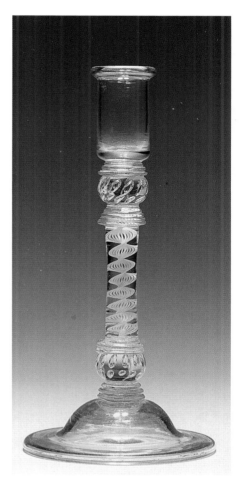

**Plate 188**  *Height 9½ins.*

**Plate 189**  *Heights 9ins and 5¾ins.*

Notable decanters (like the glorious Beilby 'BEER', plate 92, page 74 and Lynn shaft-and-globe 'WHITE WINE' have already been illustrated, plate 56, page 49. Ships decanters, touched upon on page 94, were a practical shape that became fashionable in the late eighteenth century. This rare pair with its four neck rings is unusual. It would be difficult to equal (much less surpass) the pair of shouldered magnums, plate 194 (opposite). Not only their engraved labels but also engraved decorative devices leave one in no doubt as to the intended contents. CYDER is spelt in the normal eighteenth century way. The clean lines and sweeping shoulders of such pieces put one in mind of Hogarth's definition of beauty. Flat-cut spire stoppers are the only other embellishment. New to the Collection, plate 193 (opposite) and, designed on the same lines as the above pair, is this beautifully embellished decanter, scale cut at the shoulders and carrying polished floral engraving on its body. The hollow flutes cut on its stopper are a further variant. Although one might have thought that such additional decoration was gilding the lily, you will see immediately that it works extremely well in this instance.

Another recent addition to the Collection is plate 192 (opposite), a very early shaft-and-globe decanter with a high-kick base (to lift the rough pontil-mark clear of polished table surfaces) and a stopper with multiple tears in its ball top, the peg ground in to fit. This is a very rare example of the transition from bottle to clear glass for bringing wine to the table. Next we have a most unusual and interesting group of three decanters, plate 191 (opposite) personalised with the initials M.W., carrying gilt engraved labels in the form of smiling fish, and with the centre, smaller one engraved 'THE CUSTOM'. It is possible that some day a reference may be found for these – such as a club, perhaps, or tavern. But it is more likely that they are purely personal – a family joke, perhaps. The joys of collecting are only increased by the occasional cloak of mystery.

**Plate 190** *Height 10ins.*

**Plate 191** *Heights 12ins, 10ins and 12ins.*

**Plate 192** *Height 11½ins.*

**Plate 193** *Height 12ins.*

**Plate 194** *Height 15ins with stopper.*

Frederick the Great, King of Prussia, managed to make himself popular in many lands where he travelled, and England was no exception. He was widely commemorated there through depictions on prints, porcelains, pottery and glass, plates 195 and 196 (left) media which could (presumably with official approval) reach the general populace.

Other monarchs also sought popularity in the eighteenth century, and the horse of Hanover plate 197 (opposite), here appearing on a multi-spiral air twist glass (beside a beautifully engraved floral goblet) became associated (or confused) in many ordinary peoples' minds with the rearing horse which through the ages symbolised the concept of liberty. Whether the House of Hanover actively promulgated this idea is unknown – they

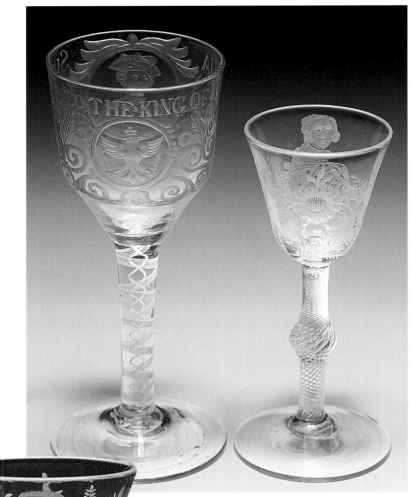

**Plate 195**  *Reverse of plate 196.*

**Plate 196**  *Heights 7³/₄ins and 6¹/₂ins.*

certainly did nothing to discourage it. Many public figures, politicians as well as princes – people of all classes seeking advancement – found glass a suitable medium for propaganda. Drinking glasses were especially suited to election campaigns, plate 198 (opposite), which in the eighteenth century so often turned into riotous drinking sprees. Shafto and Vane, like other searchers for office, probably felt that – as well as the candidates' names – the glasses carried a clearly implied promise of 'free Drinkes for ye Boyes'. Another glass shown on the right of plate 196 has a portrait of a popular naval hero, Admiral Boscawan, 'Old Dreadnought' himself, so called for his fearlessness in many an engagement in mid eighteenth century wars. Such popular heroes were often celebrated on glass, pottery and prints. But public opinion could as easily be swayed against a supposed villain or coward as it could be encouraged to support king and country – or any other cause. The glass in plate 199 (below) demonstrates this. In 1756 the unfortunate Admiral Byng, having wholly inadequate forces for the job, very sensibly broke off an attempt to lift the French siege of Minorca. But at the beginning of the Seven Years War with France, patriotic sentiment ran high. A popular outcry was soon stirred up and Byng (unbelievably) found himself accused of cowardice, court martialled, convicted, sentenced and shot, in quick order – an unpopular King gaining greatly in the eyes of a bloodthirsty populace by refusing to intervene – *pour encourager les autres*, as Voltaire wrote in 'Candide' at the time. The word 'Justice' on the reverse side of the glass to 'Swing, Swing, great Admiral Byng' (the popular out-cry of the time) seems wholly inappropriate. Engraving on glass had played its part in a darker moment of history.

**Plate 197**  *Heights 7¹/₂ins and 6¹/₂ins.*

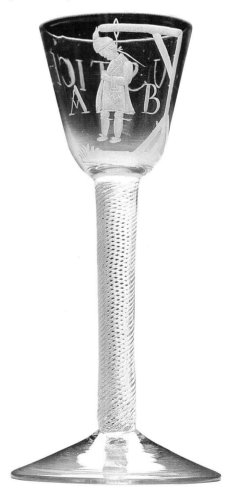

**Plate 199**  *Height 6¹/₂ins.*

**Plate 198**  *Heights 6¹/₈ins, 6¹/₈ins and 5³/₄ins.*

**Plate 200** *A monster drinking glass – surely fit for the most self-indulgent monarch – is a recent addition to the Collection, typifying the way in which it is being expanded by the addition of fine glasses. Why such giants were made is unclear. It would not have been possible to pick them up and hold them by the foot as was polite custom when drinking from smaller vessels. But perhaps some topers, royal or otherwise, simply liked large measure, since air twists and enamel twists could also be extremely large, while still obviously intended for drinking purposes. At a later date vast stemmed vessels were created which were simply footed, stemmed bowls in which to mix the punch or other alcoholic concoctions favoured by our ancestors. Height 11½ins.*

# EPILOGUE

With this book, my colleagues and I hope to have been able to give the reader a glimpse of the wonderful assemblage that is the Hubbard Collection – the genesis of which may lie in the distant past, since A.C. recently came across an interesting reference, one that may well explain his love of glass (or so his wife Penney and several friends contend). In the nineteenth century, his great, great grandfather was a director of Corning Glass Works. There is glass in his blood, so to speak. The reference is found in a book called *'The Hubbards of Sivas'* (1986). George Tiley Spencer, the ancestor in question, was a lawyer who had graduated from Yale in the class of 1837. He was "...a member of the Whig party until it ceased to exist and then a Republican, had served in the New York state legislative and had been a member of the New York Constitutional Convention of 1867. In 1868, when the now famous glassworks moved to Corning from Brooklyn, he was elected to the board of trustees".

Though A.C. himself does not subscribe to the notion, it is impossible not to speculate that this first 'gather' of glass is responsible for the formation of the Collection. But it is difficult for any amanuensis to keep pace with A.C. At any one time, his new acquisitions may be scattered on both sides of the Atlantic – and besides, the Collection is in a state of flux, being added to on every possible occasion. The only constant is its creator's application to quality and interest. Even a glance at it, however, will give some idea of the huge scope of its contents and the dedication and drive of the force that inspires it – A.C. Hubbard, Jr.

# DESCRIPTION OF THE CORKSCREWS FEATURED AS HEADINGS THROUGHOUT THIS BOOK

**Page 9**
Steel and silver, folding, attributed to Thomas Rush, English, circa 1740.

**Page 15**
Steel and silver cage with Archimedian screw, French, circa 1760.

**Page 18**
Brass and steel, folding barrel, English, circa 1780.

**Page 24**
Steel folding harp, probably from the Woodstock workshop. This type is immortalised in an oil painting by the American artist, Francis Copley. English, circa 1775.

**Page 27**
Steel, two finger direct pull, English, circa 1780.

**Page 38**
Steel and ivory dog, lacking sheath, English, circa 1730.

**Page 40**
Silver and mother-of-pearl, pocket size, Dutch, circa 1790.

**Page 52**
Ivory and steel, calendar sheath, English, circa 1790.

**Page 67**
Silver, travelling, attributed to Thomas Rush, English, circa 1740.

**Page 80**
Silver triple folding, English, circa 1790.

**Page 91**
Facet cut steel and bone, Thomason type, English, circa 1840.

**Page 101**
Bronze, Bacchus, English, circa 1850.

**Page 120**
Steel peg-and-worm, English, circa 1820.

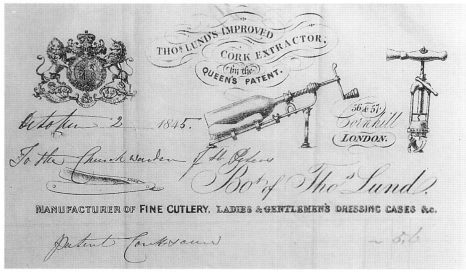
**Fig. 39** *A rare invoice from Thomas Lund, a leading corkscrew manufacturer. In the centre is an undiscovered patent design. Guildhall Library, Corporation of London.*

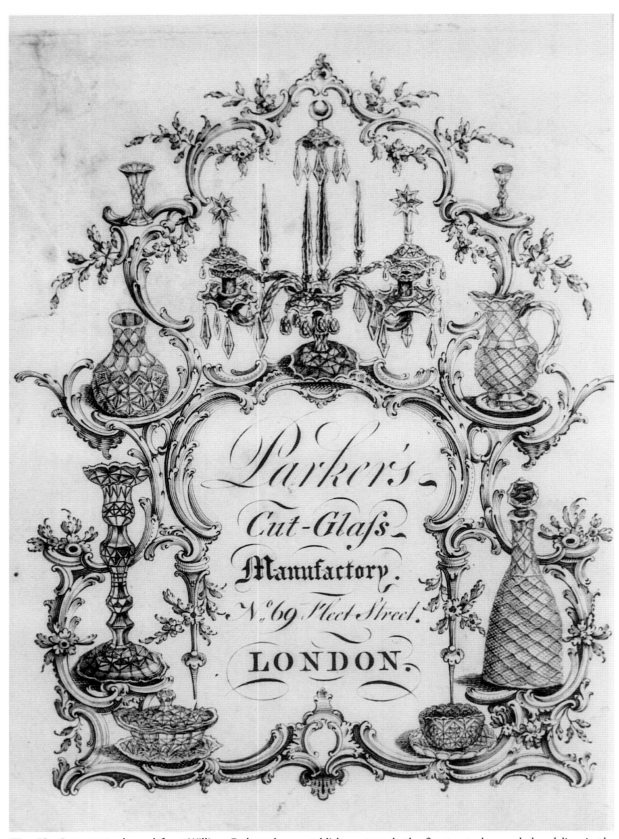

**Fig. 40** *A rococo trade card from William Parker whose establishment made the finest cut glass and chandeliers in the eighteenth century. Guildhall Library, Corporation of London.*